Crushing Snails:

An Informal Investigation into the Complex Themes of Love, Life and Creativity, told through the Analogy of a Snail.

By James Fair

Published by Grand Independent.
Blackheath Lane, Stafford, Staffordshire ST18 0AD

ISBN 978-0-9573944-2-1

For Mum, Dad, Nic, Simon, Boo and Bita.

With thanks to all who got involved, and special thanks to Peter Nottingham for showing such faith in me.

An Informal Investigation into the Complex Themes of Love, Life and Creativity, told through the Analogy of a Snail.

INTRODUCTION:

Picture the scene. It must be sometime around 1990. I am roughly nine or ten years old. It is the run up to Christmas time, an exciting time for a boy of nine or ten years old. It isn't necessarily Advent, or even a time when the decorations are out at home, it is simply the days when the afternoons are getting dark and the summer seems a long time ago. Christmas starts really early when you are that age, at least the planning phase. You have to give careful consideration to what you want (sorry Mum, '*what you would like*') for presents. This involved an elaborate process of watching the adverts in between cartoons, flicking through the shopping catalogues, consulting with my friends about what they were getting. It is a really serious process, because you don't want to be disappointed at Christmas, especially in the post-Christmas conversation when you all return to the classroom in January and boast about what you received. I can remember social status being etched in to the fabric of our childhood as much, if not more so, than adulthood. At least people can develop the confidence to reject consumerism or social peer pressure once they are a bit older, sometimes developing an identity around the rejection of it. Back then, being behind in the fashion stakes felt painful.

I am not exaggerating. I recall the glittering adverts on television that made the toys look so much better than the one I was playing with, or the catalogue where the whole collection in the range was laid out across a double page spread and made my own collection seem pitiful and incomplete. And it made no sense, because I had toys. I had loads of toys. I was not deprived in any way. My parents bought me loads of stuff, and I had my brothers hand-me-downs too. I wasn't deprived of anything. But I wasn't impervious to the adverts that said I could have it *better*. I believe the seeds of consumerism set root in the fertile minds of young children and grow into fully fledged desires and wants once we are older. We are trained to know that there is always a different model; a newer one, an extra one, a bigger one or a smaller one, a faster one or a smarter one. As a child it was fine, until someone you knew had the newer/extra/bigger/faster one. Then you felt like a second class citizen. [1]

In summary, I was an impressionable young boy in the run up to Christmas and developing my wish list of presents for Santa. The backdrop to this period of time was my parents arguing. They were going through the painful process of falling out of love, which made no sense to me then but I can empathise with it now. It was a terrible time. Evenings were either punctuated with shouting or uncomfortable silences. That's right, even the silences seemed to be awkward. I remember feeling as if it was a very precarious time, where situations could explode at any time. This meant I was a nervous little man, which I tried to hide behind a veneer of cheekiness and confidence, but I was bursting into tears at the slightest sign of any conflict.

During these difficult times, an occasion like Christmas takes on a different level of importance. Everyone must improve their behaviour in order for the event to pass smoothly. It requires effort, and the moment that any effort is involved, it raises the pressure. The pressure builds because putting in effort is *personal* and you can be judged upon it. If someone accuses you of not putting in enough effort, it is difficult not to take it personally. It is even worse if someone suggests that your effort was noble but the result was still unsuccessful, because you can't help but feel like a failure. Everyone in the house is making an effort in the build up to Christmas. My parents, perhaps conscious of the pressure that their relationship is having upon the children, decide to make an effort with the presents. My brother and I are attempting to be well behaved.

My parents may not identify with my representation of this scene, and I am happy to be corrected upon the facts. I can only draw upon what I remember, as vague as it may be, because the memory

---

[1] I am talking universally, as if everyone felt this way, but I can't be certain. I have never conducted research into whether children are susceptible to marketing or not. The fact that companies spend huge amounts of money upon marketing their products means that I assume that it is working, and creating an impact somewhere in their sales figures.

remains. I distinctly remember discovering a creative way of making an effort, albeit fundamentally flawed by childish logic. I was aware that the Christmas shopping had been taking place for a while. Adults realise this is to spread the cost throughout the year, but I did not think of that. I was simply aware that the presents were being stored somewhere, so I went off to nosily snoop for them.

My childish motivation was to find the presents that my parents had bought and then match it to my wish list, so that it would appear as if they had managed to buy everything that I wanted for Christmas! I thought they would be happy that they had bought what I wanted. However, when I wrote my Christmas wish list, it became immediately apparent to them that I had been snooping around the hidden presents, and they felt that it undermined their own attempts at making a wonderful Christmas with lots of surprise presents. The effort that I had put into trying to please them had contradicted the effort they had put in to preparing perfect presents. What is worse, is that they felt that my nosiness was simply motivated by a childish lack of patience. Whilst I was guilty of opening the doors upon my advent calendar in advance of the days they were due to be opened, I genuinely set about finding the presents in order to please them. My naïvety got me into trouble and subsequently brought about the one thing we were all trying to avoid, confrontation at Christmas time. But the key thing that has stayed with me is the memory of making that effort, being inventive to try and please someone, and completely missing the mark and ending up with the worst possible outcome. That was a steep learning curve. I was someone so young who had innocently taken the opportunity to try and be creative and yet it spectacularly failed. I think of this when I use the term 'crushing snails'.

It would be an absolute lie to suggest that I had an unhappy or deprived childhood. I was incredibly lucky and many would consider mine to be a priviledged upbringing. It would be crass to suggest otherwise and it would not make sense. After all, it was the threat of losing my happy childhood that made the divorce a particularly painful episode. If it was a bad childhood I would not have cared about them splitting up!

A huge part of that happiness as a child was the time spent creating things. My brother and I built model train sets, wrote stories, programmed games on our computer, dabbled in woodwork when Dad had the garage open. We both had furiously hyperactive imaginations that meant that we were both 'hissing'; a name our parents gave to the bizarre spouting and jumping that accompanied our individual play time. We were lost in other worlds, oblivious to reality, scoring goals for our favourite football team or fighting monsters or some other crazy day dream. This creativity was never really channelled into anything in particular. Neither my brother or I were exceptionally musical, dramatic or sporty. We were average in practically everything we did and we did lots of everything, so it was quite balanced.

When I decided to spy on the presents that Christmas, I uncovered an electronic keyboard. I was really excited but I had never really expressed any interest in playing piano or keyboard or any other musical instrument at that point, so it was incredibly obvious when it appeared on my wish list! My parents were not pushy towards me trying to learn the keyboard. They encouraged me to pursue it and they occasionally lamented the fact that I never played it enough, but it is a perfect example of the way that they surrounded my brother and I with creative opportunities. At a later date, when I was a teenager, I took a much bigger interest in the idea of playing a musical instrument, and I ended up dabbling with the keyboard after exploring both the rhythm guitar and the bass guitar.

This decision to explore music was accepted and encouraged by my parents. I believe they preferred that fact that I was a moody teenager who made too much noise with my instruments than someone who skulked off to cause trouble out of their sight. I made friends with other musicians and we creatively and collaboratively began to write songs. My teenage angst, fuelled by my percieved 'victimhood' of divorced parents, meant I had a lot to explore creatively. I put more time and effort into dreaming about that than I did my schoolwork, much to the frustration of my teachers and parents. But I got so excited about the process of creating this music, in a way that school work did not excite me. I believed that it offered a complete package of image, lifestyle and ethos. It gave me an identity. I developed confidence. How? Well nothing challenges your confidence more than taking something you have taken the effort to create and then putting it out to an audience.

People assume that artists must be self-confident to start with, because artists have something they want to 'share' with the world in a way that others choose not to. It is difficult to distinguish the people who are interested in promoting themselves from the people who are interested in promoting a message within their work. "You've got fuck all to say and you're saying it too fucking loud" was a criticism that one lecturer used to give to some of us whilst we were studying. I can honestly say that whilst I was a cheeky child, I certainly wasn't a confident one. I've always felt uneasy about promoting my work and I've always done it half-arsed in quite a self-loathing fashion, because I assume everyone thinks I'm a self-promoting arsehole. In the difficult moments of writing this book, I have felt that it seems self-absorbed, yet I am fearful of making any broader generalisations that pontificate or suggest that this book is anything else other than my own opinion. It is a strange, unusual situation. I apologetically arrive with a creative endeavour in the desperate hope that someone will accidentally notice it, like it and offer me praise, which I can politely refuse whilst glowing with pride inside. Wrestling between appearing humble and without an ego is uneasy, and people accuse you of false modesty. "You must enjoy it or you wouldn't do it" is the usual comment. I genuinely enjoy the process of making, but the process of sharing whatever I have made is horrific. So why share it at all? Well, sharing is a point of connection between different people. I've met some wonderful people who have offered their creative input into projects. If everyone created in isolation then none of those friendships would have possible. Furthermore, I believe that sharing can inspire others to engage in their own creativity. Ultimately, I'm happy if this book engages someone else in the world. I don't carry any higher ambition than that. If it inspires, great. If it creates debate, awesome. I have spent too much of my life afraid of whether someone else will like what I make or not. That is the sure-fire sign of the self-promoting artist.

In this book, I will explore the complex themes of love, life and creativity, in an attempt to explore why I do what I do, and why you do what you do too.

1. Aim:

The aim is to explore the complex themes of love, life and creativity. To explore these themes I will ponder upon the observations of a snail and the ways they are similar to our own lives.

2. Rationale:

It is difficult to define a starting point. There are so many places that I could begin. I should start with a confession. There is no narrative here. There is no formulaic starting point at which all things begin and then chronologically move forward, at least in the traditional sense of 'story'. This is a great shame for me personally, as I particularly enjoy the linearity of a traditional storyline, all chiselled and shaped to a defining point at the end when all elements converge upon a satisfactory ending. Those last twenty pages where the rest all seems to fall into place. What a wonderful feeling. Am I deliberately denying you such a sensation? I hope not. I wouldn't want to rob you of these delights. My aim is certainly to satisfy! But I cannot promise the linearity. The problem lies in the subject matter. I've chosen to explore these ideas and concepts in the form of a sham investigation. Why? Because it would otherwise become a sprawling myriad of digression.

On occasion, I feel that I am not doing very well at love, life or creativity and I feel the need to reflect upon these issues. I use the word 'feel' because I'm purely talking about an emotion or my perception, as opposed to a fact. Many people would argue that I'm doing fine in life as an English speaking white male and that I'm fortunate enough to be born with a distinct advantage in this ethnically nepotistic, unequal society. I'd have to agree, and it would be unfair to pretend to be seriously struggling in life when I obviously have the time to ponder on the existence of snails as opposed to digging a field for a living or some other physical hardship. Some critics may argue that I've already uncovered that my uncertainty over love, life or creativity is a very first-world crisis to have, and arguably an unnecessary and self-indulgent one. I think that these issues are universal and uncertainties about them may plague all humans on the planet at some stage. So, why am I not writing a book about the world's inequalities instead of one focussed on the individualistic conditions of self-fulfilment? Well, I'm not sure that love, life or creativity should be considered individualistic conditions, despite the fact that they are being *sold* to us as such, and many of us are treating them as such. I'll go into detail later, but I think that my insecurity is not unique to myself, and in many ways others, especially companies, deliberately induce insecurity in order to sell us the remedy.

Why snails? Well, it's a long story, but I guess we have time. I've spent the last few years working upon a series of films that are collectively called 'The 72 Project'. The premise behind this project is that it is possible to shoot and edit a whole feature film in three consecutive days, i.e. 72 hours. My reason for pursuing such high-speed production belongs in a different book, but this research does mean that I have been concentrating on the process of snipping corners and looking at ways to accelerate things in filmmaking. This acceleration, fuelled by technological change, is all around us within society. Email is faster than the old fashion post, or 'snail mail'. We have video on demand, we have microwavable food and we have mobile phones. We don't like the notion of 'waiting' for anything. Don't get me wrong; I'm not a 21st Century Luddite, as I benefit from a lot of this technological change and I utilise a great deal of it. But it also frustrates me on a couple of fronts. Firstly, I not convinced that technology is wholly responsible for the accelerations that we are witnessing, as I think it is *humans* that design technologies to streamline the necessary *human* effort. We design things to make things easier. However, the human effort never seems to disappear, it only seems to be *displaced*, and we find ourselves working harder than ever before, keeping up with the communication and the information overload. Secondly, I loathe the fetishism that surrounds technology. I find the relationship that people have to their mobile phones fascinating, especially the constant need to update versions of their phone upon a contract, presumably because the technology is becoming 'obsolete'. This forced 'technical obsolescence' by manufacturers is such an unethical practice that it is hard to believe that society stands for it. But their ability to infuse their products with abstract meanings through advertising means that hordes of people try to remain at the cutting edge of technology so that they are the best technologically equipped citizen in their circle of Facebook friends. Bizarrely, the people who use the weather app on their phone never seemed to carry a barometer with them ten years ago, arguing that it's obviously easier to check it on their phone than it was watching the weather forecast at the end of news broadcast on a standard definition television. The fact that these technologies are manufactured using the finite resources and materials that our planet has to offer means that many of these technologies are badges to demonstrate one's vulnerability to technological fetishism, placing abstract values above the actual value. Our ability to access a weather forecast instantly isn't nearly as important as the fact we're holding minerals in our hands that are mined in war-torn countries or manufactured in sweatshops.

So, choosing a snail is a deliberate attempt to focus upon something that is natural and universally recognised as slow. If this reason for focussing on snails seems unsatisfactory or tenuous for you, then I quite simply propose that the snails are a lateral leap and I don't need a reason to choose them. By using the analogies of a snail as a lateral leap I don't need a reason as to why I am choosing a snail, as that is the whole point of a lateral leap. It doesn't have to make sense. I wouldn't bother continuing to read the book if this bothers you, as it's quite a fundamental part of what is still to come. This whole book is based upon the observation of a snail and how we can laterally leap to other thoughts and constructs from that starting point. It didn't have to be snails, it could have been scissors, cactus plants or lemon juice if needs be. It just happens to be a snail, so get over it.

3. Theoretical context:

Love, life and creativity. Three things that I want to be good at but I'm not sure I even understand what they are. I've occasionally read different things about each of these subjects but researched none of them comprehensively, and therefore nothing that I have read has wholly satisfied my curiosity. Whilst I'm perfectly capable of reading further into any one of these areas, it seems to me that no one has even grappled with the basics very effectively. Liars write books that claim to simplify these subjects, but these are complex themes that are open to interpretation. For example; I've often used 'love' at one end of a simple continuum whereby 'hate' is at the opposite end and 'like' and 'dislike' are somewhere in the middle. It looked like this:

LOVE – LIKE – DISLIKE – **HATE**

However, previous girlfriends didn't enjoy being wedged in between crisps and holidays on the simple continuum and argued that 'love' is more complicated than that. I'm still not convinced that it is. My first port of call when struggling to define anything is a dictionary and I am reliably informed that love is an "intense feeling of deep affection". This would fit with my continuum theory. But I have seen signs and bumper stickers that say 'God is Love', which doesn't really fit into my continuum theory. Either the Christians are lying (which I believe is against their religion), or my understanding of love is inadequate. This is the rationale for undertaking this research.

Defining 'life' is even harder than 'love' as it is a far larger concept. Love is a part of life, which also includes many other things. It is possible to be completely biological about life; it is the condition that distinguishes animals and plants from inorganic matter. Living things grow, reproduce, function, change and eventually die. This is very matter of fact and pretty unequivocal. The problem arises when we search for a *meaning* behind life. Some authors, like John Gray, argue that there is no meaning, we are animals, we reproduce and consume the environment that surrounds us, and he believes that we'll consume until it can no longer sustain us, so humans will die. This is a fairly bleak outlook, and seems incredibly deterministic. We don't seem to have a choice over our destiny under this theory, so we may as well forget any effort to save the planet, as the destruction is inevitable if we continue to expand as a population. The traditional sticky-brick is *consciousness*, which differentiates us from plants and other animals and has allowed us to develop constructs such as 'time'. We have histories and futures, and these are part of our lives, and the part of life that I am interested in researching in this book. It is our 'consciousness' that will hopefully save our planet. Obviously there are many philosophical contributions in this field of study and it would be impossible and pointless to go through them all here as it's been done before many times. I'm interested in looking at life through the prism of a snail. If it throws up some similar philosophical contributions then we'll take a temporary detour, but I'm not interested in battering you over the head with lots of metaphysical musings, largely because I don't know many myself and because it is a bit heavy for what I had in mind. Let's keep it light people! If you want a philosophy book, go buy one.

Creativity is part of life too, but can also be considered a pre-requisite to life. After all, humans are created through intercourse between a male and female. This broader definition of creativity may frustrate some readers, but I think it is essential that we put as broader frame as possible on the term 'creativity', so we don't limit the scope. On the face of it, creativity is quite easy to understand, because it means producing something and bringing it into the world. But does this apply to everything, or is there a caveat? Surely the word 'original' should be included there also? Bringing something original into the world? I think of my time as a child copying cartoon characters from my comics. I could copy them, but I wasn't *creating* them.

"Nothing is original anymore!" I can hear the pessimists scream. This is rubbish. This is the unimaginative response that an artist will come up with when confronted by criticism of their creativity. The prolific film maker Robert Altman argued that he was not original, just stealing bits from other filmmakers and fusing them together. I think this is the essence of originality, being influenced by others and using it differently. The ability to think independently and creatively, and the quality of being novel or unusual. If you don't take this as the definition of original, then perhaps nothing is 'original'. Even then, there are many things that have not been discovered yet, that will only be done so through small steps of technological evolution. Obviously I cannot list them here or I would be the godfather of their creation. But let me list one: an underwater cinema. Now, you may think that this idea is absolute rubbish. There is no need for an underwater cinema. I don't think so either. But there isn't much of a need for bungee jumping either, but it exists to pleasure people. My underwater cinema is fundamentally flawed because water plays havoc with the properties of light. But I figure there is so much interest in underwater film making and nature documentaries that people could go down and watch movies whilst drawing air from an oxygen tank. It would be a memorable experience, more so than watching some dross in the cinema.

You are probably thinking this is a terrible idea. And you would be right. But as a starting point, and one which could be developed, we could find ourselves at lots of different ideas just from the initial process. Going with the first idea might be stupid, but if we refined it, and went with a hot-tub cinema, or even a sunbathing cinema, then we may be getting somewhere! The sunbathing cinema would be projected beside the swimming pool for all those people who hate having a holiday where they are expected to sit beside the pool, yet that is what their partner wants to do. Instead of having an argument on holiday or having to go their own ways during the day, putting a movie on beside the pool might work. You are probably thinking that is a poor idea too, albeit marginally more feasible than the underwater one. What about an outdoor film festival much like the way that music rock festivals are run? A holiday and cinema taken from the sunbathing idea. Memorable experience and event taken from the underwater idea. I have always thought this would be quite feasable. I think some people are already starting to do these things, which is like most good ideas, people arrive at them at a similar time. For example, the start of cinema was highly contested between different groups of people around the world who were developing similar technologies at the same time.

Creative thinking is a process not a result. A lot of the time we only judge originality on the difference of the product instead of the process. There can be great originality in the way that something ordinary is achieved. An example would be a regular painting, which we criticise for being unoriginal. But when we are told that it was painted by someone using their foot, we begin to see the brilliance. How original! At this point, the unoriginal painting becomes the whole point of the exercise. You were not meant to believe that it had been painted by someone's foot. I attempted to achieve this once within filmmaking by making an entire feature film in 72 hours. The audience weren't supposed to notice the difference from any other film. It was the process that was original, not the product.

Is originality essential to creativity? Is knitting creative if you are copying a pattern yet making a jumper that didn't exist before? Is cooking creative if you are making a cake but you're being instructed by a recipe? This is part of the complexity that I am hoping to explore within this book.

Similar to love, life and creativity, plenty of stuff has been written about snails. These books are trustworthy, because snails are tangible and not open to much interpretation. However, not much has been written about love, life, creativity and snails in relation to one another. Therefore I think I have discovered a niche in the marketplace, and something 'original'[2].

---

[2] Unless you consider Patricia Highsmith, a writer and alcoholic who never settled into any lasting relationship and kept snails as pets. Maybe nothing is original.

4. Method:

The primary method of exploring this spectacularly hard topic is through casual observation and informal, un-rigorous reading. I will also critically reflect upon instances in my own life that I believe may be relevant to prove a point. This is by no means scientific, and I apologise in advance if this disappoints you. The problem with taking a scientific approach to the complex themes of life, love and creativity is that it is difficult to identify a suitable method of inquiry, based on reason and yielding empirical and measurable evidence. I could pretend, and say that I have been ethnographically observing snails in their field (pun intended). For the scientifically minded, this would offer some demonstrable rigour to the rest of this book, but I am not willing to pander to your needy demands. Put it this way – why don't you conduct your own scientific investigation into how 'love' works and see whether you still have a partner at the end of it? I'm exploring these topics for the sake of it, and for my own enjoyment and enlightenment. I confess now that I am addicted to the puzzle, and intend on spending the rest of life trying to discover what I enjoy. I fear that uncovering the *actual* mechanics behind love, life and creativity would leave me taking it all for granted. I remember playing for ages as a child with the magnets on the edge of the fridge. I loved how they invisibly repelled one another. This was all fascinating until I learnt about magnetism in school, and they quickly became uninteresting. There are tonnes of things that surround me on a daily basis that fascinated me as a child that I now take for granted. Some of them I still can't understand scientifically, but having had someone explain it to me scientifically at some point makes me feel stupid if I continue to demonstrate any sense of wonderment or curiosity. I am supposed to understand that there is no such thing as magic. I guess the purpose of this book isn't to explain anything to you, but to encourage you to get this childish fascination and curiosity back. To want to watch snails and think of how fascinating they actually are, instead of taking them for granted. Or aeroplanes. Or mobile phone technology. Perhaps ignorance is bliss? We don't need to know.

Except ignorance is not bliss. Power resides with those who *do* know. I think the problem is that we have become specialists. Employment has become sub-divided into specialisms, so we only concentrate on our little corner and subsequently engage with other areas without any understanding of how their role works. We don't need to know how the rest of the world works, as long as it remains to do so. Yet the public become shocked when scandals are uncovered within work practices like the recent phone-hacking in journalism or the derivatives market in banking. As these scandals unfolded, we heard about 'corrupt cultures' as if scores of people were performing malpractice on an epic scale, yet far more likely is that a handful of people were performing in an unethical manner and others had no idea of what others were doing because it wasn't their specialism. For example, the teller in your local bank most likely played no part in causing the international financial collapse (although is probably paying the price through being made unemployed as the banks 'restructure'). Most tellers probably can't explain how the convoluted economic practices of traders work. Even the mortgage lenders within your local branch, who most likely lent money to unsound customers, most likely did so upon the recommendation of higher management, with no idea of how and where the *actual* money came from. Similarly, the service team who bring you drinks upon aircraft probably don't understand the physics behind flight. They certainly don't get paid the same as the pilot, so why should they need to understand it?

But we are responsible for our own life, love and creativity and we should want to understand about these things. Businesses are encroaching upon these areas of our lives and offering their services in order to simplify the world for us, but often with much larger ramifications. Big supermarkets offer all the products under one roof, but often with no consideration for the local impact. I remember witnessing the decline of the high street in the town where I grew up, as the butcher, the baker and the grocer all shut when the supermarket came to town. The consideration of 'food miles' was a distant thought at that point, and we happily ate food from all seasons despite the fact it had flown in from parts of the world that we had never even travelled to. I never really considered it either, but my dad was working for the supply of milk to supermarkets, and was constantly under pressure to see costs cut. Local factories closed and milk travelled to super-factories. I was vaguely aware as a child that the milk on my cereal was political. My dad took pride in my political awareness of the milk industry, and spent a fortune buying some delicious milk that came from a dairy in my hometown.

I digress. I was meant to be discussing methodology. I will use the snail as a metaphor, obvious and obscure, to leap laterally into other subjects. For those who are unsure or who need to be reminded, a metaphor is a type of analogy, where I can draw comparison to some element of a snail to some other part of life. I guess some of the comparisons here would also qualify as an allegory or simile, but let's not get bogged down in the rules of language.

To support my casual observation of snails I shall be including photographs from a recent project that I developed. Their inclusion is meant to offer two things: a visual stimulus to break up the monotony of text and a chance to look at something different and reflect upon your thoughts for a while. I don't know about you, but I do find that I often whizz through a book, casually *reading* the text but not necessarily *savouring* it. Yes I *read* it and *understood* it, but did I *really* get it? I think of all of the texts in the world where I was momentarily inspired or elated, but quickly converted that enthusiasm into reading further instead of stopping and reflecting for a bit. Then, as I reached the end of these books, I had an overarching sense of 'that was a good book', as opposed to the specific moments that lodged in my head. I can think of one exception and it involved a picture. I was reading Alain de Botton's 'Status Anxiety' in which he wrote about architecture and how it reflected the dominant value systems at the time of building. He gave the example of churches and cathedrals quite literally built as temples of wonderment, architecturally designed to inspire and induce awe. He ended the chapter with a photograph of the Canary Wharf skyscraper in London, with the logo of a giant banking corporation written on the side. Nothing needs to be said, we can see that our dominant value system is capitalism, or most likely corporatism. The effect of this picture punctuated the flow of text, and I was propelled into thinking about what had just been read.

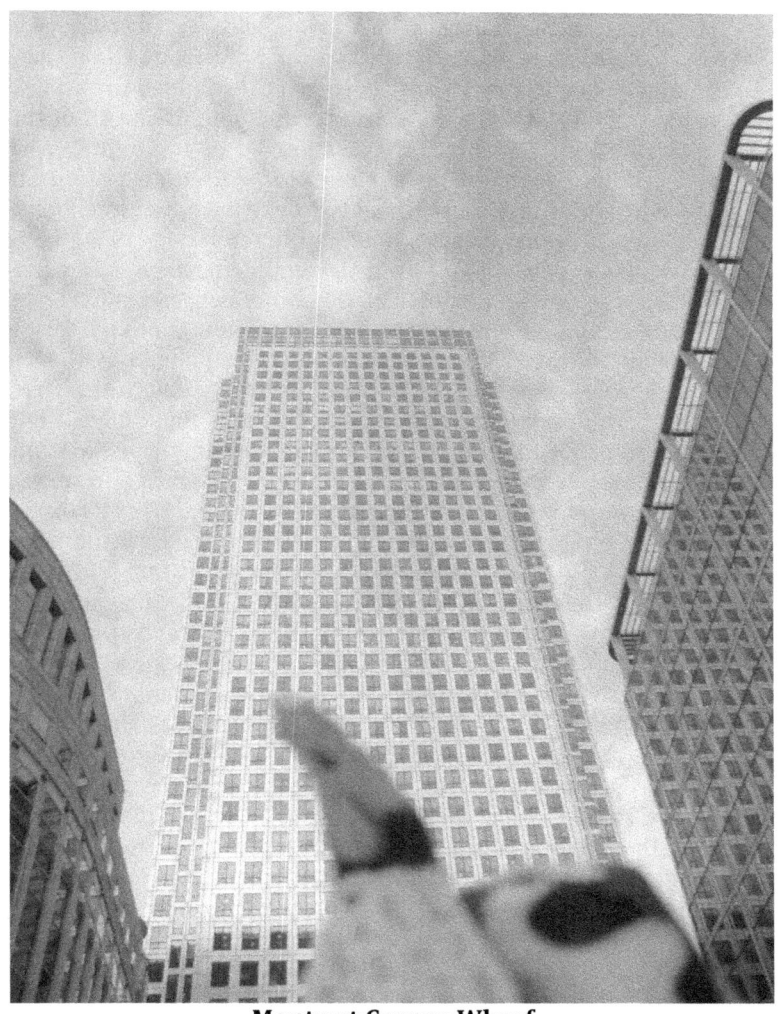

Monty at Canary Wharf

Another part of my methodology was to release snails into the world. These weren't real snails, they were papier-mâché, and built out of letters from my bank that told me I was overdrawn on my overdraft and therefore they would be charging me some more money for the privilege of having none. I have spent all of my twenties and early thirties wrestling with the financial burden of studying for two degrees and living with an over-active social thyroid problem which means I cannot resist the temptation of going on adventures with my friends if the opportunity arises, even if the fragility of my bank account can't support it. All of this has been a source of much frustration to my parents, who are constantly annoyed at my inability to live within my means and therefore my subsequent inability to pay back multiple loans from the Bank of Mum and Dad. Now, at the tender age of 32, as I feel I reach the end of my arrested development stage, I can begin to think about paying them back. This process hasn't started yet. The phenomenon of arrested development is undoubtedly couched in selfishness, whereby an individual is overwhelmed by the need to *live* their life, opposed to merely surviving. Day-to-day activities must be infused with meaning, as if all jobs must have a purpose other than facilitating the treadmill of paying bills. Victims like myself believe a job must have an identity attached and serve some higher purpose than simply making money. This is of course absolute bollocks, but it takes a while for the reality to kick in. I'm not advocating the curmudgeonly grim view that life is a hard grind and then you die as the people who peddle this viewpoint are misers and should be avoided at all costs. They suck the enjoyment out of you usually with a crushing cynicism that prevents them for seeing any positives. They are exhausting people. What I am advocating is the discovery (or rediscovery) of simple things. I believe my arrested development was due to the overwhelming amount of individualistic corporatist ideology that I swallowed whilst swimming in their shiny pool of consumption. I believed that the shiny computer would make me creative and all the gadgetry would support me in my busy lifestyle. I never once considered that I wouldn't be so busy if I ignored all the gadgetry. As I developed, and overwhelmed with the sheer volume of communication, I appreciated the value of time away from it all. I realised that it didn't matter. This may sound like a ludicrous epiphany to have, and some people may be thinking that they are already ahead of my recent discovery and that I am an idiot for only realising it now. I implore you to stop being so smug. Our education systems, our politics and our media are all geared towards peddling individualist ideologies. Being susceptible to its allure is not uncommon, and no one should take pride in being the first to uncover the sham behind this hollow culture, because the smugness and pride are an extension of the problem. People who take pride in their counter-culture position make the counter-culture position an obnoxiously pretentious place to reside for regular people. Yes, I'm using the word 'regular' because this is the one thing that many counter-culturalists believe they are not. They are defined only in opposition to culture, and mock the 'regulars' as 'sheep'. I actually view this as an extension of the same toxic individualism, albeit an inverted position. The counter-cultural position is as much of a badge as the goth, the chav or the hoodie. Conforming to non-conformity and all that. No, the correct position to take when discovering the falseness of our consumerism is not lofty smugness, but a passionate dedication to the municipal discovery of simple things. Don't smirk when someone has his or her epiphany because it is degrading to all involved. Offer to celebrate by lying on your back and watching stars together, or some other simple pleasure. There is nothing greater than the sensation that you have uncovered the simple things and that you have someone to enjoy them with. No one will enjoy anything with a smug arsehole.

Sending papier-mâché snails out into the world reinforced my sense that there were kindred spirits in the world. I sent some snails to friends to take photographs and I left others in shops and bars for strangers to discover. My friends helped to paint the snails, and I wrote labels that went around the neck with the following text:

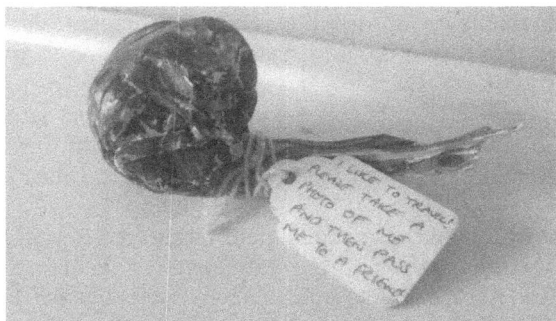

I like to travel, take a photo of me and pass me to a friend.
Email your photos to crushingsnails@gmail.com

As these photographs began appearing in my inbox I felt a warm glow. It is difficult to describe this sensation other than excitement. I was excited that people were engaging, taking part in a simple project with no rewards or prizes, just the idea of contributing. This act of participation demonstrates creativity on so many levels. Most obviously, there is the creativity of framing a photograph with a papier-mâché snail in it. But secondly, and perhaps more obliquely, the act of sharing it with me, and subsequently the world, is an act of creativity. I say this because the dictionary definition of creativity is to actually produce something and bring it into the world. Whilst this doesn't necessarily mean sharing something (you can create something for yourself if you wish), the sharing of the photographs means that the contributor is actively involved in creating a collection of photographs from different collaborators. Not sharing would simply be creating a picture of a snail. But sharing is creating a bigger thing.

All that remains is to start listing the observations that I made whilst watching the snails and then thinking of ways in which I can reflect upon love, life or creativity. Easy really. I personally find that watching snails is a fascinating experience. I am mesmerised by their movement and the physical make up of their bodies. The fact that we share a planet with these strange creatures creates a sense of wonderment in itself. When people state that "there's got to be more to life than this", they are oblivious to the incredible good fortune that they exist upon a rock that is floating in space that happens to support 'life'. The mix of chemicals and conditions means that a thin band of distance, from the bottom of the sea to some point in the sky, carries all known life forms. It is easy to forget how incredibly rare humans are in this galaxy. This is a classic problem of perspective, and it is difficult to reflect upon our good fortune on a daily basis, especially when bills need paying.

When watching these snails, I am interested in breaking down my observations into different categories. The first category is the physical nature of the snail. What can we learn from its actual body? The second category is the behaviour of the snail. What can we learn from its functions? The third and final category is the representation of a snail. Away from the actualities of snails, what can we learn from the representations of snails? These three sections make up the basis of my research.

5. Research:

5.1. The physical nature of a snail:

5.1.1. The trail:

Let's begin with something that isn't even a part of the snail itself, but is something they leave behind: the trail. The 'snail trail' is made of mucus, which the creature produces in order to facilitate movement. It simultaneously acts as a lubricant so that the snail can move softly across surfaces, whilst also acting as glue, so that snails can climb and stick to perpendicular angles. It is interesting to note that these functions are almost diametrically opposed in our minds – a glue to stick you to something whilst also letting you move smoothly. We tend to consider glue as a method of holding two elements together instead of facilitating movement. We consider lubricant for ease of movement, but you wouldn't rub your hands in lubricant before attempting the climbing wall. This multi-purpose mucus presents us with our first opportunity to laterally leap across our topics. Does love share any qualities of this mucus? Let's leave the sticky 'love' out of it for now, and keep some semblance of maturity.

Arguably a good lover should give their partner freedom whilst simultaneously providing support. The nature of that freedom need not be specified here, and would differ from relationship to relationship. I'm not advocating swinging or infidelity, rather a freedom to pursue personal goals, perhaps sporting, artistic or professional. Providing support alongside this freedom is quite demanding, but essential. If someone that you love is truly engaged in pursuit of their personal goals, then they will most likely on occasion be susceptible to feelings of self-doubt or stress. Supporting your loved ones through these moments can feel hideously un-gratifying, largely because they are 'personal' goals, and if the person involved doesn't like it, they should stop. There is nothing worse than trying to help someone who is self-inflicting pressure upon his or her own self. It is a difficult conundrum, because you have to balance many factors into this situation. Is your partner being realistic about their personal goal? If not, at what point do you let them know they are being unrealistic? What if they are being realistic but suffering too much as a consequence? Maybe they are neglecting you whilst they pursue the goal? There are many variations upon this situation. In much the same way that I cannot point out the balance between the stickiness and lubricant nature of snail mucus, I cannot specify the balance between freedom and support within a relationship, I only believe that both should be present.

Delivering support can also be perilous in some relationships, with some people feeling inadequate if they constantly require the support of their partner to succeed: "I want to do this for myself!!" This somewhat infantile position is exacerbated by another concern from our childhood; we are no longer subject to unconditional love. The days where we could shit on the walls and still be considered cute are long gone (in most cases). You're not going to get a raspberry blow on your belly if you accidently stick your fingers through the speaker cone of your lover's hi-fi the same way you did to your parents' as a toddler. Your lover will go mad, and rightly so. Unlike the mucus on a snail, the blend of support and freedom must be reciprocated. This is the complicated part and most probably the part where relationships fail. Not only must there be a balance between freedom and support, there must also be a balance between giving it and receiving it. It is tough to find someone in this world who can do all this with you and still press all your buttons. I know plenty of relationships where they haven't achieved this balance, and one partner is constantly downtrodden or overshadowed by the other. These people are either too sacred to be alone or they quite simply don't have any personal goals of their own to pursue, so don't really require the freedom. This tipsy balance is probably far more common than my utopian version above, and probably why I haven't yet settled in a marriage. Of course there is one overarching factor that can compensate for the lack of balance in any relationship: *understanding*.

Understanding is a useful term. In some relationships it can be used as a synonym for *acceptance*, regardless of whether it is understood or not. For example, I know a woman whose husband plays golf every weekend whatever the weather, and she accepts it. She doesn't understand golf, or why he would go out in the rain to play it, but she accepts that he wants to play golf and grants him the freedom to do so. This tolerance can be called understanding. Understanding can also mean agreement; inasmuch as people can have an 'understanding' as to where the boundaries are in the tolerances of their relationship. I-cook-the-food-and-she-does-the-dishes-kind-of-thing. Bizarrely, using understanding as the opposite of ignorance and meaning that you 'comprehend' is not always apparent in relationships. It never ceases to amaze me when a partner says that they don't know what their lover does for a living or does with their time off work. I believe this kind of freedom in a relationship is tantamount to not caring, and there may be infidelity lurking somewhere in the equation.

Let's move on. What can the snail trail tell us about life? On a most basic level, the trail points to where the snail has come from. It is a visual representation of their immediate history. Try to imagine what it would be like if these trails were visible for ourselves. It isn't too hard to imagine, because my mum often caught me out for walking into the house with muddy feet. There on our carpet would be a track record of where I had clomped through a room. If I had dirty hands I would leave fingerprints on our white cupboards too. This would really piss my mum off. But seriously, imagine if our long-term histories could be laid out behind us for an omnipotent view from above, like our view of a snail trail. We would be freed from the tyranny of narrative fallacy or warped perspective. This is one of my biggest bugbears with learning history at school. We went through timelines of dates, making causal links between things that happened, never fully exploring the complexity of any given situation. As Rob Newman pointed out in 'A History of Oil', the escalation of Franz Ferdinand's assassination to the First World War always seemed a bit extreme, but set against the backdrop of the Berlin to Baghdad railway and the growing industrial tensions of Britain, Germany and Russia, it all starts to make a bit of sense. The maxim is that the victor writes history, usually from his or her own perspective. It is contaminated with self-interest and lack of alternative perspectives. Societies or individuals do not look at history from the omnipotent view of a timeline despite this being the preferred visual representation in history books. Instead, we look at history from the standpoint of our own perspective, with events shrinking in size according to their position and distance from the eye towards the vanishing point. Every new event changes the perspective of what we saw before. Things that are closer in time are fresher in the memory and influence the way that we perceive the major events in the past. Smaller events in the past drift into recesses of the mind and are only recalled in pub quizzes or reunions. I don't believe that personal perspective is a problem at all, as long as we can try to see from the perspective of others too. It is the externalisation, the objective viewpoint, which can so rarely be achieved, but should be strived for.

The snail trail is a visible demonstration of the route that the snail took to get to a certain point. I like to think that this can be interpreted as the journey or process that one takes when being creative. I remember being frustrated in maths lessons at school, when I gave the right answer but didn't get a mark because I could not show my 'working out'. I could not demonstrate how I had got to the answer. Without the trail, I was either cheating or it was a fluke. Whilst this frustrated me at the time, I have come to realise the benefit of processes, especially if we are to understand our mistakes or develop repeatability. The process of development and the pursuit of improvement is not an easy thing to market and sell. We like to have an idea of time and effort involved. I think of the adverts with a hideously muscly man stood next to a thinner picture of the same person, and the caption 'Get the perfect stomach in four weeks!'. Now, the reality is that whilst this is achievable, it is not achievable without some kind of sizable effort. Furthermore, for those who have the perfect stomach, it was the sizable effort that makes them proud of what they have achieved. If we could all look like that with no effort it would be meaningless.

We are quick to want a payoff from our creativity. It is difficult to accept that original thoughts and good ideas do not always come easily. The process of reflection and consideration are often dispensed with in the hope that the first thought will do. Often this means it isn't all that well developed and mistakes occur a bit further down the process. I see this a lot with student filmmakers. They often don't develop their scripts to be that original. They mimic and imitate the styles of their favourite films and make substandard copies. This is less of a creative process and more of an act of forgery or plagarism. It is quite common for someone to copy and imitate the style of their favourite artists without going through the development and process that the originator went through. That is why some artists consider originality and innovation as the core value of their work instead of perfection. Their work will be copied and perfected by imitators who are looking to be like them and improve upon it. These imitators will always exist, but it is incredibly hard to keep creating original work. The process that the originator went through is the snail trail. The visible path from the origin. As I work in education, Bloom's revised taxonomy is often cited for the identification of learning outcomes, which are divided into three "domains"; Cognitive, Affective, and Psychomotor (*knowing/head, feeling/heart* and *doing/hands* respectively). The belief is that within these domains, learning at the higher levels is dependent on having attained prerequisite knowledge and skills at lower levels. In other words, before you can *create* something, you need to be capable of understanding, analysing and evaluating it.

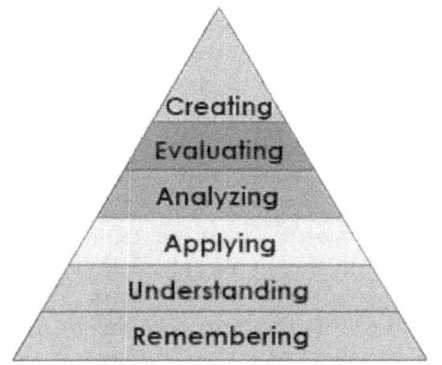

**Figure 1 Bloom's Taxonomy (Revised),
with American spelling of 'analyzing'.**

Whilst my first instinct is to believe that we don't need to be capable of understanding, analysing and evaluating something to be creative, I realise that it certainly helps if you can use these skills to unpick your creativity. In his book 'The Medium is the Massage', Marshall McLuhan argued that the amateur can make bigger leaps in creativity than the professional because the 'expert' always accepts the groundrules whereas the amateur can work freely. He cited the Beatles as an example of people who made a giant leap in music despite not being trained professionals. This is true, and their creativity (and originality) is undoubtable[3]. However, whilst they may not have originally understood the genius of what they were creating, they were certainly capable of repeating it. And subsequently listening to their interviews in the years that followed, it becomes apparent that they had analysed their own music in the process of developing it. It is therefore this process of analysis and reflection that I believe seperates the creators from the imitators.

The key thing about this visible pathway is that it demonstrates the effort that we went to in order to achieve something. Effort is the exertion of physical or mental energy. I don't believe that people really value effort, despite what they sometimes say. I believe that they really value effectiveness. For example, putting in the effort to woo a lover is only worthwhile if it pays off and is effective. Not being effective hurts because it indicates that your effort was not good enough. When people say "at least you made the effort" they are saying it for your sake and usually because someone else has not valued it. Effort is the means, not the ends. You make an effort to achieve something else. If you have to be rewarded for the effort it is usually because you can't be rewarded for the end result. "Well done for trying". "It was the taking part that counts". I was annoyed in maths if I had the right answer but the 'working out' was missing, because I felt it a calculator was still effective, if not reliably more so than my own mental arithmetic. The difficult and discouraging thing about creativity is that effort is not rewarded by an audience as much as effectiveness. I know plenty of really talented and skillful musicians who lament that they cannot make a living the way that some teenagers can in the music industry. Or talented artists who are not considered good enough to get their work into national museums and then find themselves confronted with a row of bricks or a tent with condoms on it and say to themselves "I could of done that". Or authors who have written great stories yet find they are not published as easily as some

---

[3] Postmodernists will argue that it is questionable, as The Beatles didn't invent new musical notes or chord patterns, they simply fused previously existing styles into a new form, borrowing from all over musical history and putting it in one big melting pot. I believe the process was original and it arguably led to a new way of approaching music. I'm not getting into postmodernity here because I'm writing a book about love, life and creativity told through the analogy of snails. Which in itself is a postmodernist thing to do.

trashy airport novel. Then there are film makers, all of which argue that the true film makers are not recognised within mainstream cinema. Each of these examples are the people who are making an effort that isn't proving to be effective in the eyes of the common person. Perhaps creativity is only effective when audiences collectively confer acceptance of the work? This public acceptance or act of endorsement by others means that the art has been *recieved*. Does failure to be endorsed by the world at large mean that our creative efforts are no good? No. Arguably some of the audience aren't looking for creativity anyway, they are looking for entertainment. And they are rewarding the work that entertains them effectively. Society doesn't really reward effort that much; just effectiveness. Critics say a movie is bad and give it a one star rating; giving little or no consideration to the time it took the producers to get it on screen, not to mention the thousands of other filmmakers who didn't even get as far as the screen.

Creativity does not have to be measured against the expectations of others as it has a personal value to ourselves. The process of being creative can be as important as the thing that we create. The effort we put into something can be more of a valuable experience to us the result itself. Sometimes, I have discovered more about myself from the projects that have failed to be effective despite my best efforts, and the effort has been an invaluable personal experience. We tend to judge our creative endeavours in the eyes of others because our society has other dimensions which depend on communal approval. But our independent creativity does not have to conform to communal approval, especially if we do not wish for it to be consumed by others. And on many occasions; the best examples of creativity exceeded what the community was prepared for anyway, most notably the fields of science and technology, where we have witnessed changes in the way that society thinks and behaves as a result of giant leaps in original thinking. Creativity doesn't have to win over an audience, and you should never let the fear of acceptance stop you from being creative. Society's celebrations of success tend to mean that we don't value failure. If we paid failure the equal attention as success we would be celebrating all the time. Not a bad idea. It sounds stupid, because failure isn't something we should celebrate. But we should recognise its value. Failure is often a fundamental stepping stone in achieving success. Success cannot happen without the existence of failure and potential of failure is what makes success a sweeter achievement.

Often failure teaches us more about ourselves in any given situation than success. It is a painful process of recognising weaknesses. We don't want to confront our weaknesses as we believe that they are flaws in our character, as opposed to accepting they are part of our character. In other words, they are weaknesses because we label them as such. Like success and failure, weaknesses are the opposite of strengths. We like identifying our strengths, and often we build our character in the direction of what we are good at, whilst trying to avoid our weaknesses. I hated maths in school so I dropped it as soon as I could and built a career towards never having to revisit it. At a later point, I realised I really enjoyed learning maths, I just didn't like being *taught* it. I didn't like the idea that I was studying it to be regurgitated in an exam. I wanted it to be applied and relevant. At a later date I saw the way that maths was interwoven into all kinds of subjects, and the compartmentalised method of studying it was the weakness. Of course this is my opinion. Other people loved the way that maths was in a subject of its own and really excelled at it. This is the point. Strengths and weaknesses are subjective. I know people who are really optimistic, positive characters who never say 'no'. This is a virtue, but others will label it as their weakness. They may be labelled as naïve or unrealistic for taking things on when they should have otherwise rejected them. I'm not suggesting that we scrap the labels of success or failure. They are useful, but they should be recognised as being subjective and not fixed terms. If this was a cheesy self help book, I would be encouraging people to look for the positives in any given situation. It is certainly a question of perspective. The cynical view of doing this is that we are lying to ourselves not to deal with the pain of failure. This is not the case. We are simply thinking about what things can be salvaged from the pain of failure, and if nothing can be salvaged, then the fact that we have thought about it is a positive in itself. The real pain lies in the place where you don't feel you can confront failure.

The way our culture celebrates successes means that we should hide and forget about our failures, or they become personal weights around our necks. People hold us accountable for them.

Yet overcoming failure to eventually succeed is an incredibly rewarding experience. The sense of a failure contributing to the success is a relief. The pain wasn't in vain! But sometimes people are too quick to escape in the face of failure instead of spending time analysing it and working out how it may contribute to the future. It is unfair to say that this is giving up too easily or not putting in enough effort. It is fair to say that the effort hasn't been very effective. We live in a results-based society where success is championed. Few people care if the process has been worthwhile but the outcomes are not successful. Record companies don't keep the artists who aren't making money, even if the 'artist' has developed in the process. They need the artist to make money and so all other values, from artistic development through to the value of failure, are not recognised. Trying out new ideas may fail commercially, but it may also yield results of a different kind, or be successful in other ways. Not experimenting means we will never find out.

I think a classic example of this failure to experiment is ironically reflected in the majority of the so-called 'creative industries' in the UK. What does that mean? Are they truly creative? The subsidies suggest that they are not innovative enough to survive. The term 'creative industries' is applied to companies who are making things usually in the broad field of media. This is a shame, because there are plenty of other creative industries, for example weapons manfacturors who sell weapons to both sides in a conflict like Libya, but these are not considered creative. Instead, the term is reserved for companies who generate or exploit knowledge and information. Under this term, a lot of people who consider themselves to be working in the creative industries would be redundant. The idea of exploiting knowledge is obvious. There are few industries that can exist without exploiting existing knowledge. Generating knowledge? I'm not sure that many can lay claim to that.

Those companies that can genuinely lay claim to creating new information and intellectual property are certainly the hub of the knowledge economy, but there are plenty of smaller firms that cannot distinguish their niche. They saw that the tools for digital creativity were plentiful and decided that they could exploit it by providing services for people who have neither the time nor the creative confidence to make websites, take photos or shoot films themselves. Their assets lie in the fact that they can make something just two or three steps ahead of the common man. This is less about the originality of thought and more about the being ahead of common understanding. I am not belittling this; most of business is about trading a skill for a price because someone else doesn't have the time. I don't bake bread, so I buy it. I'm not saying I can make bread the same as a baker, because they obviously have more experience than me, but I struggle to believe that every baker is an original one, each with their own nuances. Most of us are consuming mass produced bread, made by machines to create a continuity of quality where ever we bought it. One loaf should taste the same in London as it does in Belfast. The same expectation is created around the creative industries. A television show should work the same in all the territories that it gets shown. It should follow conventions and genres. So that is hardly creative. Yet they should be distinguishable enough from the rest of the programmes that went before so that you are not watching the same things all of the time. Similar, but not the same. There lies the creativity. Being the same but different is at the core of most of the creative industries.

As a film maker, this is apparent in the movie industry. Genres and stars still make money for studios, which means they still pursue them. Despite the fact that the apparatus of cinema can no longer bring in the same revenues and profit margins that it used to, studios are still determined to defend their library of 'assets' than reconsider what their assets may be. Working out what their new income stream will be would be the greatest leap of original creativity for a generation of otherwise lazy filmmakers. My criticism about the creative industries in the UK is that neither the process or the product is particularly creative or original. We still operate in very conventional ways in order to fit in with a 'global' industry at large. The UK film industry is not a creative industry, it is an imitation industry. Risk averse and a copy of the Hollywood model. Like a snail trail, it is visibly connected to the past.

I find it fascinating that creative industries are growing in economies where traditional examples of industry have disappeared as a result of outsourcing manufacturing to countries with cheaper labour. In the societies where creativity and original thinking is supressed, it can surprisingly have the opposite effect and people find different ways to express themselves. Is our culture of affluence the death of our creativity, despite the fact that we all seem to think that we are engaging in it more? A paradoxical growth of creative industries in the countries who don't need to demonstrate originality to survive. Isn't that how we've come to rely on subsidies for arts? I'm making a huge assumption and one for which I will be criticised. Art doesn't need to be profit making. Giant advances in originality have resulted outside of the economic realm. Absolutely. But a creative *industry* based on subsidy? It is like the answer to the maths question without the correct 'working out'. Yes it is easier with a calculator (subsidy), but can you work it out for yourself?

At this point, the list of economic and cultural benefits of supporting the arts usually get wheeled out. The production of movies brings money to hotels, locations and caterers for example. Galleries bring tourism. Once again, I agree. But this indirect subsidy therefore isn't strictly for the creative industries alone, it is for their subsequent spend elsewhere. It is a prop to industry as a whole in the belief that the cultural elements will increase civic pride and stimulate spending in general. This round about way of spending money in the creative industries means that the demands for how the subsidy money is spent impacts upon the creativity of the project. Projects must fulfill pre-requisite requirements that by default, limit risk and therefore originality.

I don't wish to get into free market economies or whether the state should be involved in the elements of society that cannot or should not be monetised, but I believe that our subsidy structures in the creative industries are to combat the fact that there is an American cultural dominance and monopoly and in order to compete we must subsidise. It is a pointless war that can only be lost, because meeting them on their terms, within their structures and apparatus, means that all other competitors will remain marginal. Until these competitors can find an original way to differentiate themselves from American cultural hegemony, the subsidies will remain a contentious issue for years to come. And I wonder whether we will appreciate the cultural value of these artefacts when we no longer have a pension in the future. Maybe then we'll see where Governments needed to intervene, and where they did not need to bother.

What else can this snail trail teach us? It can be interpreted that we are connected to our past, our origins and surroundings, and we are part of a larger journey that is evolution. If we accepted that our creativity was a process that has no fixed end, that it is evolutionary and changing as we change, we may be more willing to accept our own work. This process connects us to our surroundings in a way that we have been grown unaccustomed. Our lives have become fragmented, to perform roles within larger organisations and societies. It is rare that we are connected to products or projects from concept through to completion. Think about food. It passes through so many hands on the way to our plate, often having travelled further than many of us could ever hope to travel on holiday. Perhaps this alienation from the things that we consume means that we don't appreciate the real value of these products. The idea that we just purchase our products instead of having any involvement in their creation has become pervasive. In the 'developed world' we are consuming more of everything, food, fuel, media, you name it, we are consuming it in greater volumes than ever before. But are we valuing it less? We take more photos as a result of cheaper cameras. We listen to more music as a result of mp3 players. We play more games and watch more movies. But are we getting the same experience from these things? Is the reduction in personal investment resulting in a reduction of value?

I think computer games are a really interesting example. I remember playing River Rescue upon my Commodore Vic 20 computer. The graphics were crude and there was only really one concept to the game, to rescue people stranded on a pier. As the levels increased, the speed became faster until it became difficult to control the boat. Nowadays, this game would be embarrassingly poor for even the oldest mobile phones. But at the time, it presented me with enough challenges and excitement to sustain my attention for hours. As computers improved and games became more complex, I found myself becoming frustrated that games would require more and more of my time to complete. The simplicity was a value for me. The emphasis for computer game development seemed to more interested in photo realistic graphics and complex gameplay, but these required less of my imagination. Similarly, movies have been driven by technological fanciness and photo realistic 3D animation but arguably require less imagination. Perhaps we have become passive and less involved in the content. It becomes less about playing the game and more about admiring their technological complexity and 'newness'.

Perhaps we don't want to have to use our imagination. We used it in the past because we had to, but new products will not only save us time, they will save us the effort of imagination too. Some people are relieved at the idea that we don't have to keep rethinking everything. It is probably a relief for many that we have news channels and TV shows that do the thinking for us and just tell us the answers. "Thinking so you don't have to" was Ze Frank's tagline on his humourous video blog. These shows take in all the information and analyse it and feed it back to us in an understandable, concise chunk. That is the theory anyway. There are many disutopian novels that have been written about the bias of such media and the world in which none of us think for ourselves any more. We become almost like bacteria or animals, just existing in idleness. I am not advocating or promoting either of these philosophical positions, it isn't why I am attempting to write this book. My belief is that we are different from animals exactly because we can think and are conscious of time. We have histories and futures and we can consider abstract thoughts. Considering the many abstract thoughts that are possible is enough to challenge the greatest minds into thinking creatively. A refusal to use our imagination and not think about the consequences of our actions is a refusal to use our mind to its full potential.

Recognising the value of our imagination is difficult. It is difficult to quantify and measure new ideas or concepts that are not present to the senses. Yet being good at using our imagination is of great value. Imagine what it would feel like if I swung a golf club really hard onto the end of your chin. Being able to imagine this pain is better than experiencing it. Using a combination of experiences and perceptions, your imagination uses the word 'IF' to develop new ideas in the safety of your mind, a virtual world where you can imagine the consequences. It is surprising how little this imagination gets used, when people don't think through the consequences of their actions, either because the complex variables of 'ifs' become paralysing, or because they simply don't feel the need to use it. Some people refuse to imagine the consequences of things that are not immediately apparent, like if we run out of oil. Others spend all their time imagining a world without oil, and are busy trying to secure the next source of energy. It is this leap of imagination that may save us all at some point, in much the same way that it is the failure to use our imagination that may kill us all!

Our imaginations are under assault from a number of distractions that require our thoughts and senses. The emails, the text messages, the status updates. All this information takes a temporary meaning and is of fleeting importance, and it serves as the same distraction that my old computer game did, for absorbing imagination to picture simple things. As we move towards more visuals and photographs, like a tagged photograph to illustrate the bruise on your leg to all your friends, the imagination is used less and less, as it is all there to see and sense without having to imagine it. Watching the movie instead of reading the book. Consuming more, thinking about it less, and arguably reducing its value to us. I think we should consume less and value the things we do consume, and take time to appreciate our lives.

I'm starting to pontificate, and I can't stand that. It's very pompous and veering towards to the smug counter-culture crowd. Let me throw away the beret and pick a counter viewpoint, just so you don't write me off as a socialist or communist. It's possible to interpret the snail trail as an example of individualism, as snails very rarely seem to travel in pairs. The trails show that paths cross, sometimes over the body of another snail. I have seen little evidence to suggest that they follow one another. These are unique journeys. Ultimately, all our lives are our own. Whilst we may choose to share our time with others, we essentially have our own thoughts, our own opinions, our own desires, goals and prejudices. Sometimes we climb over others (metaphorically mostly, sometimes literally) to get where we want to get to. It is extremely unusual to find a truly selfless person, if it is possible at all. I won't go into individualism too much here, as I would like to develop these themes far more when addressing the solitude of the snail shell. Instead, I think it is suffice to say that the snail trail shows individual paths that sometimes cross, and they can represent multiple interpretations for love, life and creativity.

At this point I'd like to spend some time reflecting on the adventures of the papier-mâché snails. Whilst they never left a continuous trail of slime behind them, there was a series of images that emerged from some of the snails as they were found and collected by friends or strangers, and pictures started to emerge of their adventures. This visual trail is much like our own collections of photos from the past, which flag up our previous experiences and capture them for a later date. At this point we are confronted by a truth. "Oh my God I was so young then, look how we dressed!" At this point our memory is exposed as the malleable liar that it is, shaving the edges off of pain and increasing the excitement of the happy times. Old romances may seem alluring again and nostalgia for people and places can swell your mind. If only a photograph could capture our thoughts and feelings at same time as the flash goes off, we could truly recognise how time has changed us, beyond aesthetics.

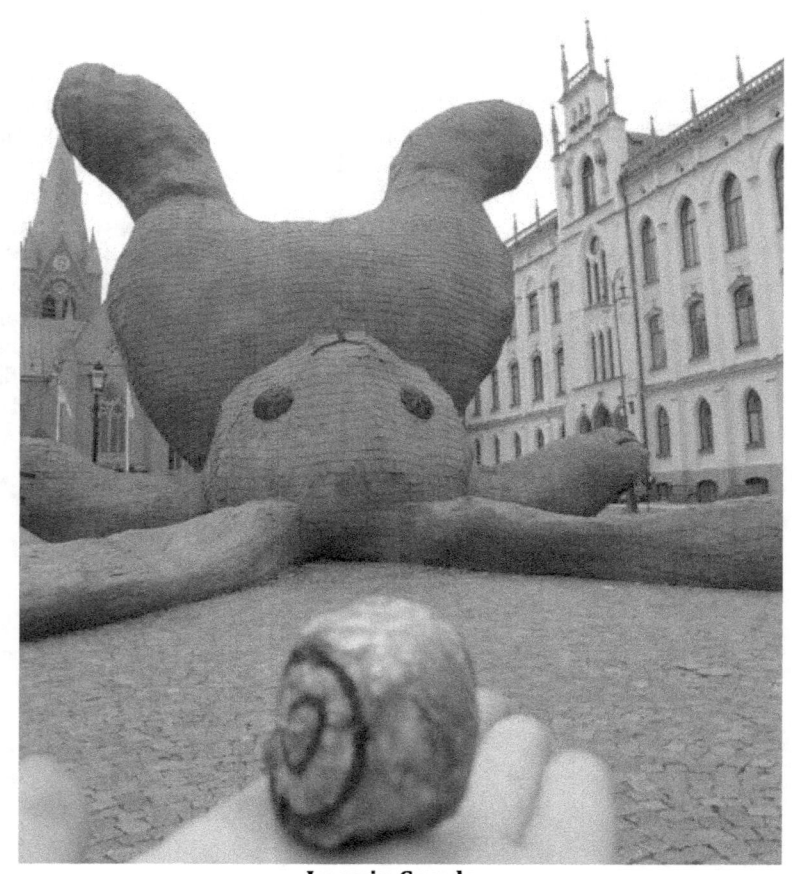

Lucy in Sweden

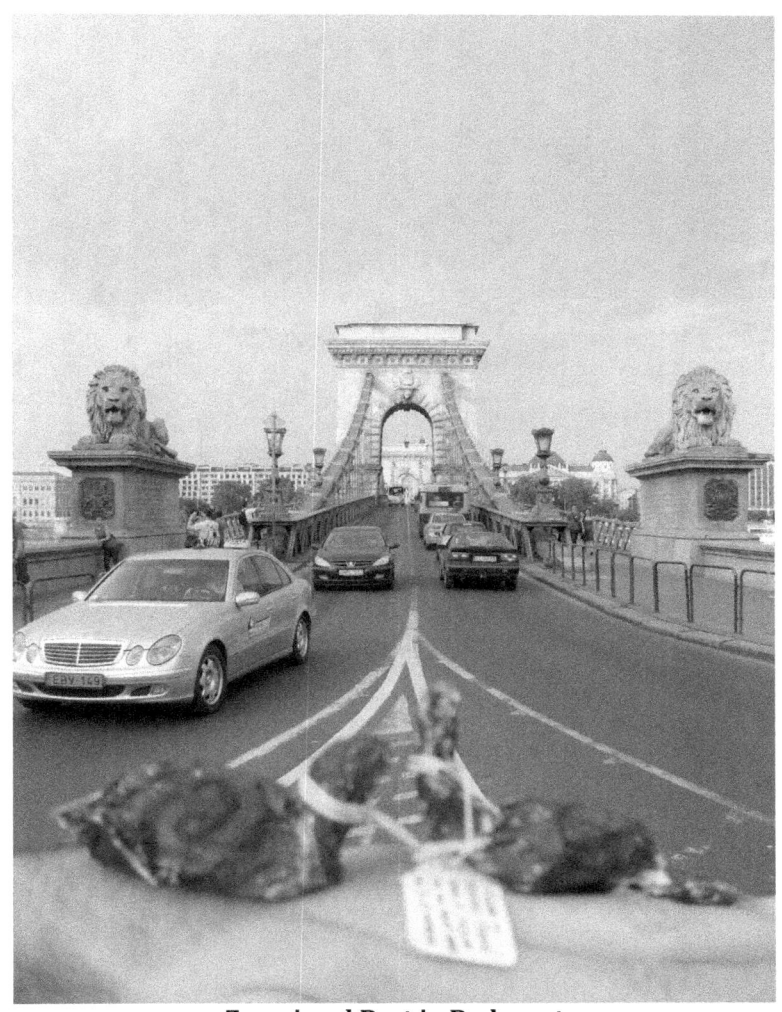

Zsuzsi and Bert in Budpaest

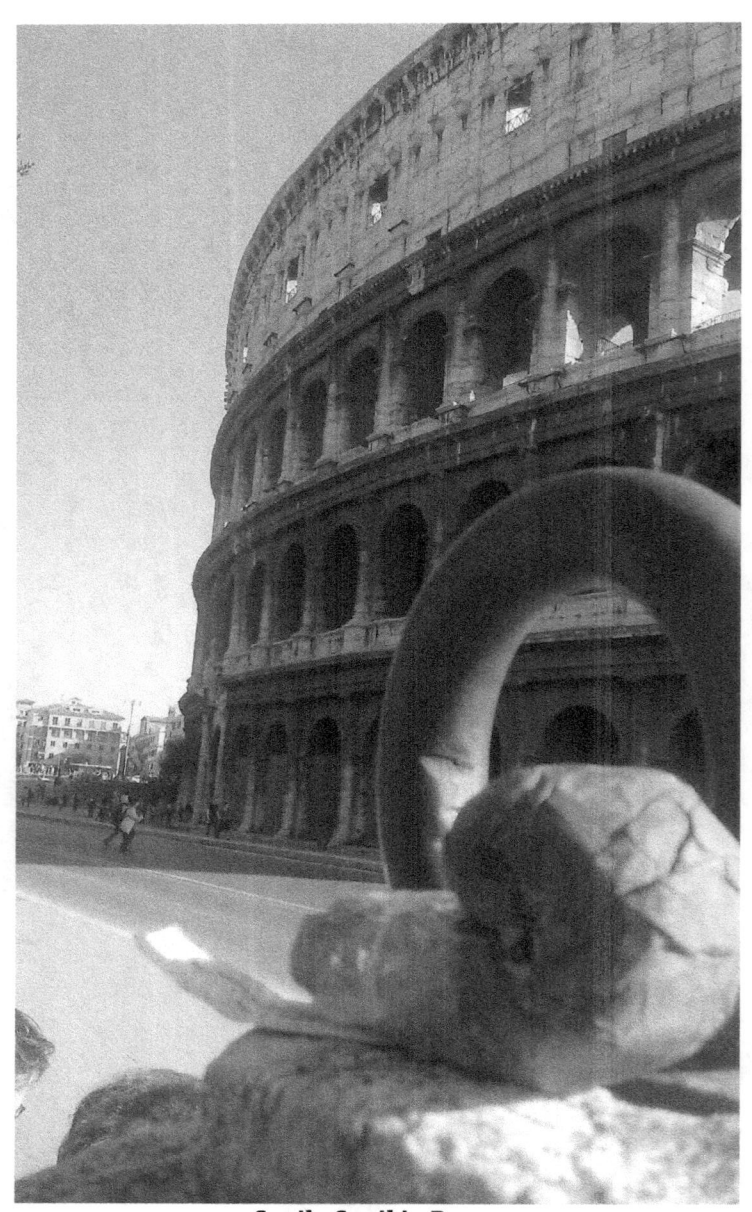

Snaily Snail in Rome

5.1.2. The shell:

The shell is the most iconic and obvious image that we consider when we think of a snail. The trail may be called a 'snail trail', but it can also belong to slugs. On land, the shell is largely the domain of the snail, but in the sea there are plenty of shell creatures. The shell is an exoskeleton, which protects from predators, the heat of the sun and from mechanical damage. There are tonnes of biology books that can go into the exact nature behind the growth of the shell, but we're not interested in that here. Just like the trail, we want to see where we can laterally leap from the understanding of a shell.

Let's start with an obvious connotation: the shell as a home. Whilst we like to think of the shell as a snail's home, it would be more suitable to think of it as a mobile home. Whilst the shell is fixed to the snail, the snail determines where it will go. In this sense, snails are like travellers; nomadic creatures that have all they need on their back. One of the most precious status symbols in the 'first world' is the possession of a fixed home, one that is usually bought with the help of a bank lending you money that you will spend a sizable chunk of your life paying back. This mortgage has an influence on your life. It determines whether you can afford to just drop everything in the world and go somewhere else. Obviously, the wealthy can buy a few houses and skip between each, but the majority of people struggle to pay for the one they have, or kind-of-have, because really the bank owns it. Our relationship to our homes and our belongings is strange. Unlike the necessity of the shell, we connect ourselves to all sorts of belongings that are not essential. We attach all sorts of different values to our property, from a monetary price through to a sense of identity. Like the shell, we make them an extension of ourselves. This isn't strictly exclusive to homeowners, as renters also attempt to make a space their own (albeit they sometimes furnish their spaces lightly, knowing they may take flight again soon). Most of us are making an investment in our homes: financially, emotionally, or just through simple time spent cleaning it. We admonish those who don't make investments in their home precisely *because* we believe that the home is an extension of the person, in the same way that the shell is a part of a snail. If someone is messy at home, it says something of his or her character. Conversely, the same is true if the house is meticulous. Our justification for investing in our homes is quite simple; we are going to spend so much time in it. We include the things that we like and enjoy. We try to make them comfortable. Home sweet home! However, not everyone lives alone like the snail. In many homes there are multiple people, often families, sometimes housemates. At this point the home becomes a bit of a turf war and our personal space usually gets relegated to being a room within a house. Even this can sometimes be shared with a partner. This concentration of humans into one space has the capacity to emotionally explode at any point and can sometimes be a fractious experience (it can also be a harmonious experience and there are examples of 'happy families'). A snail doesn't share its shell and has the freedom to move its home wherever and whenever it chooses. By contrast, our fixed home and the people we share it with, has an impact on our lives that can sometimes create the feeling of captivity. Home is not always the sanctuary but sometimes the source of the problem in your life.

The same can be said of a snail too though. Whilst the shell is actually designed to protect the snail, it can also be a source of weakness because it reduces manoeuvrability. Other creatures can squeeze into places that a shell may prevent. Unlike the slug that can hide under a rock rent-free, the snail is tied to the shell and all the exposure that comes with it. Our homes are the same, for as long as we attach monetary or emotional values to our homes, we are forced to care about it. I envy the people that have reached a nomadic state of existence and have no fixed abode or possessions, but it is so alien to modern culture that it seems difficult to even contemplate living that way. There is such a dominant ideology of home-ownership that seems to have developed from when humans stopped being nomadic and started 'settling', that to continue wandering in this day-and-age seems freakish. It is usually identified as a selfish act that an individual goes through, considered political, destined to be deliberately lonely. The stereotype is that they have rejected all need for possessions and 'belong to the land', which cannot be owned. If this position is taken by a white, educated person then we ridicule them as part of the smug counter culture that I described earlier. If it is a black aborigine in Australia then they are given second-class citizenship. We are so indoctrinated to believe that ownership of land is necessary that anyone who doesn't own land is an outsider. I'm not talking about whether you have bought a property or you rent one, because both are contracts that give you 'ownership' of your space. I'm talking about homelessness, which is a status defined by a lack of something else. But our system of living means that the home is proof of your existence. Want to set up a bank account? We'll need proof of your address. Want to take out library books? We'll need proof of your address. Want a mobile phone? Proof of address please. It is a cycle; few jobs will take people without a bank account, which won't take people without an address, which requires money for rent, for which you require a job. Alternative titles for homeless people demonstrate their position in society. A vagrant is a person without a settled home or regular work who wanders from place to place and lives by begging. In ornithology a vagrant refers to a bird that has strayed or been blown from its usual range or migratory route, and is called an *accidental*. If you lose your home due to disaster then you are 'displaced', which is a posh word for homeless and once again defined by your lack of 'place'. Destitute means you are abandoned without the basic necessities in life (of which home is considered one). Each of these words suggests that homelessness is against the norm, despite the fact that none of us are born into the world with a shell on our back. Interestingly, if you can't make payments on your belongings then you are not dispossessed, the bank repossesses. This means you never owned it in the first place, which is completely true. Until it is fully paid, you have just been approved on the probability that you have the means for payment. Let's take a break and look at where those papier-mâché bank statements travelled.

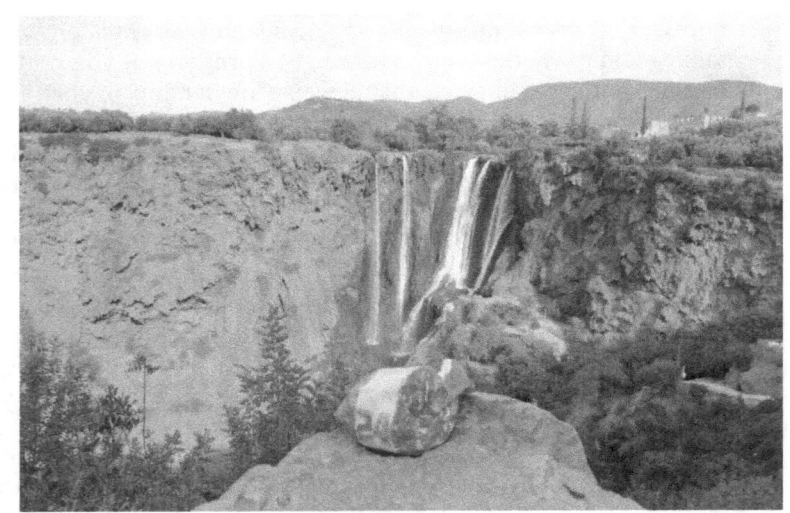

En Xeïc in Morocco

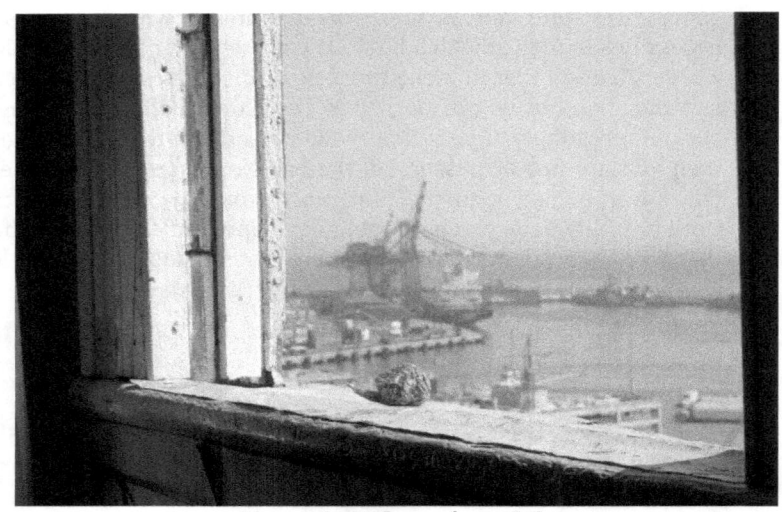

Ginger in Valparaíso, Chile

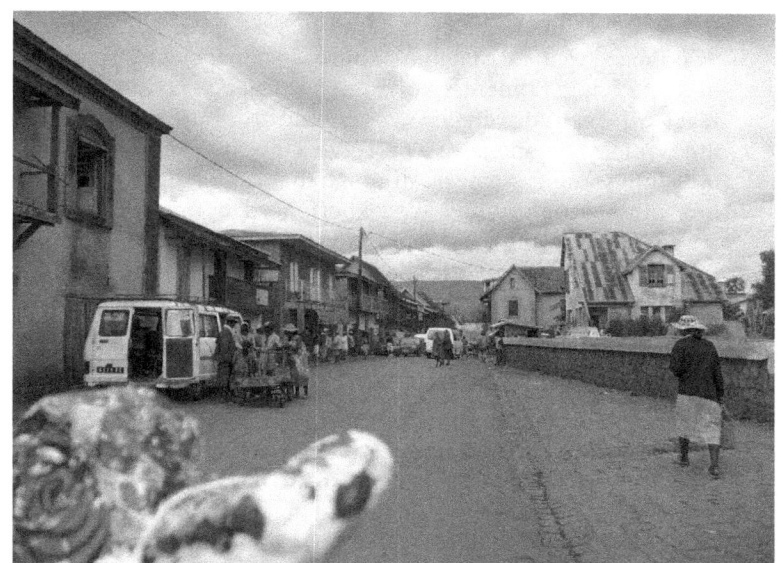

Indri in Ambavalo, Madagascar

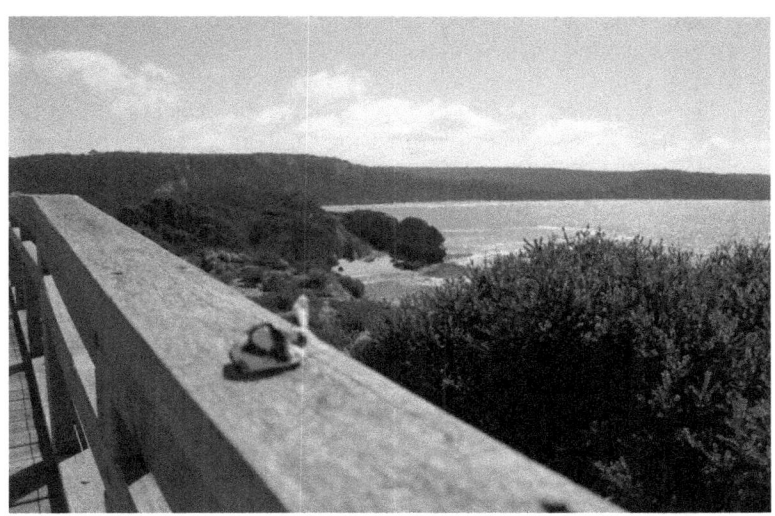

Monty on the Great Ocean Road, Australia

In life, the shell can be considered to be a metaphysical protection as opposed to an actual one. Whereas we have considered the idea of a shell as a home, let's consider it as a sanctuary of our self, a place of mental refuge. We retreat to our personal defence mechanisms whenever we perceive a threat or intimidation. This is not simply about shyness, although that can be the extreme case. In life, most people will have experienced a time when they feel personally uncomfortable and the sensation changes their manner. I witness this on a regular basis if I ask students to contribute to a lecture by asking me questions. With 150 people in the room, not many feel confident about putting their hand-up. Some people speak up simply because it is preferable to the silence. Others whisper to their peers, but don't want to be so un-cool as to ask the guy at the front. Put some of these people in a smaller group and you can't shut them up. I guess this is actually part of a far larger conscious construct; the ego instead of the id as Freud would describe it. Our ego is the shell that we wrap around our id to prevent grief and enable long-term benefits. I'm not going to pretend that I possess anything more than a rudimentary understanding of psychoanalysis, so I won't develop much further along this line. Suffice to say; in life we all construct metaphorical shells around our character.

Let's move on to creativity. I believe the process of being truly creative is to emerge from this shell and express ourselves to others through some medium or another. It is the threat of ridicule or humiliation that often prevents people from pursuing their creativity any further than is minimally necessary. When anyone points out your creative weaknesses, you can quickly feel inadequate. It may be a teacher, parent, partner or friend, the effect tends to be the same; you want to stop. I believe it is because the courage of bringing something creative into this world can be intimidating. The fear that people won't like it, or understand it, can be petrifying. Hence the emotional reward for getting something right is quite high, and it feels great when there is applause or even a slight sign of appreciation. Some artists like to say that they carry on with conviction that someone, somewhere, will 'get' it, or that it is for personal reward and everyone else can get lost. This has certainly helped me at some of my many low points, but the reality is that without an audience, it all seems a bit pointless. Some people assume that being creative is an attempt at vainglorious narcissism, especially if the creative person is seeking an audience to see their work. I've always felt this opinion is quite cruel, and tends to come from quite bitter and cynical people. I'm not denying that there are people who seek approval and social acceptance through their 'creativity', but these 'creators' don't tend to be wholly engaged with their field and are instead interested in imitation. Perhaps it is the internet or the explosion in self-publishing that has lead critics to assume that anyone who makes something is self-obsessed. This is absolute nonsense, as the process of creativity has incredibly therapeutic ramifications, both for the creator and potentially the audience. Personally speaking, I find that the commitment of taking an idea and altering it into something that can actually exist in reality is incredibly fulfilling, and the process has had equally fulfilling experiences for people that I have collaborated with. Creating the snails is a classic example. I love the fact that I have turned these bank letters into papier-mâché snails and then asked friends to decorate them and send them around the world. In twelve months the blog had 14000 hits, and over 200 likes on 285 posts. The project was worth it even if the joy spread no further than the occasion that I sat with strangers in a pub in Dublin and decorated snails. This collection of people, who turned up out of curiosity after I posted on the Couchsurfing website, spent one afternoon doing something completely random that very few others in Dublin were doing that day. The same could be said with my friends who met to paint snails in the Spotted Dog in Birmingham. The experience was something different for us all, a break from the humdrum of our regular lives. That is the therapeutic nature of creativity; it helps break the repetition of normalcy. This also gathers criticism, because a further assumption is that artists have a problem with normalcy, and that we must see ourselves as being above someone else. This isn't the case. Wishing to break from the norm isn't exclusive to creativity; most of us pursue the same sensation when we take a holiday.

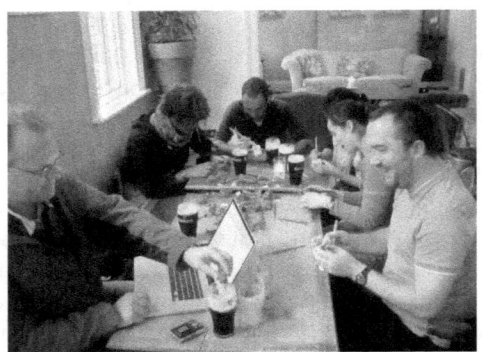

Snail painting in Dublin...

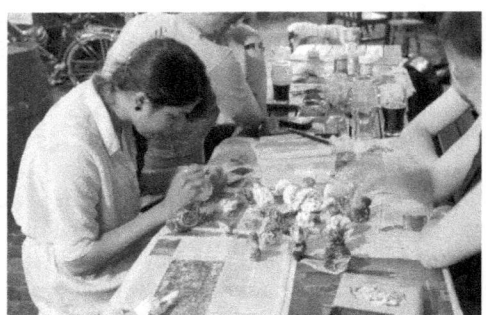

... and again in Birmingham

Releasing something creative out into the world is a scary process. There is an assumption that you enjoy the experience, otherwise you wouldn't do it. Whilst there exists a cliché surrounding the tortured artist, cynics assume that the tortured artist is as much as a performance as the art itself. Another manifestation of the self-obsessed, vainglorious narcissism mentioned earlier. This again is unfair. Critics seem to believe that there is a necessary need for balance in the world, whereby anything created is fair game for criticism. The logic is as follows: Artist wants to share art to make a living; therefore the artist is subject to the volatile nature of the marketplace and therefore criticism. If an artist chooses not to take art to the market it is either a) crap or b) a vanity project. Both of these approaches also merit criticism. Therefore nothing is impervious to the reach of criticism.

Criticism isn't completely bad as it can be an incredibly useful tool for analysis. At its best, criticism can be an intelligent commentary that actually fosters debate and furthers understanding. But there is also a strain of criticism that hypocritically carries all of the characteristics it seemingly loathes in others. Some critics need to sell papers (commercial mainstream) and they seek audience approval (vainglorious). My personal bugbear is the internet trolls, whose belief that everyone is entitled to opinion in the same way that everyone is entitled to create. I don't disagree with the freedom of opinion, but the thought that goes into their criticism doesn't often match the thought that goes into the process of making something. The balance is wrong. A filmmaker or musician can spend years working with a team to make one thing, and it can be criticised by hundreds of people who listen or watch it in an instant. It is for this reason alone that being creative is the equivalent of coming out of the shell. A snail's shell can protect them from some of their predators. Withdrawing inside the shell can provide shelter from immediate harm. Whilst a snail can hibernate it obviously cannot live its life entirely in the shell. You can probably see where I am going with this clumsy analogy. "Oh yes James! We try to protect ourselves from creative criticism by retreating into ourselves! What a clever use of analogy!" I hear you whisper. Actually, I think the thick layer of mucus that a snail uses to traverse over sharp objects is probably a better way of describing how we should deal with creative criticism. We shouldn't withdraw into our shell, we should learn to gloss over thorny issues and carry on regardless. Actually, my analogy about snail shells was to illustrate that we are all capable of withdrawing, even without the presence of creative criticism. Fear makes us withdraw. Not just fears of criticism, but also fear of violence and fear of ridicule. It sometimes feels like we are surrounded by a climate of fear that seems to encourage us to withdraw. I believe that being able to express yourself creatively, using whatever media or outlet you choose, is an important part of our personal development. It takes bravery to bring any form of creativity into this world and it should be respected. It is easy to be destructive and far harder to be creative. Let's also note that the shell is weaker when the snail is younger and still developing. It is constantly developing and gets stronger as it gets older. So let us recognise development too, and that a shell doesn't just pop out of a snail's ass on the third birthday. It *grows*. And creativity should be seen likewise. When everything else is trying to be instant, craft can sometimes take time.

I remember being made to feel inadequate when studying art at school because I couldn't master the techniques that were considered the objective benchmarks of good art in the examination. I accept that if I were to become an *artist,* I would arguably need to master such qualities. But I enjoyed art because I could express myself with it, and if people didn't like it, then so be it. I understand that school was teaching skills that may of helped me to express myself through art, but part of my enjoyment was that it was instinctive, not instructed. I have studied filmmaking to the point where I struggle to enjoy it in the cinema. When I go back to art, it is because I want to be childish and naïve again. I am hoping that people can recognise this as a quality within what I am doing with these papier-mâché snails. One of the paradoxes of studying something is that you become so fixed in the methods and modes within the field, that it is difficult to develop original thinking on top of what has already been discovered. I mentioned Marshall McLuhan earlier, as he pointed to the huge leap that the Beatles made in music despite not being 'experts'. He also made the case of Michael Faraday, who made his discoveries without formal education. McLuhan's belief is that we are looking backwards when we study something and it prevents us from making the necessary lateral leaps for originality, because we accept the ground rules of our study. The logic behind accepting these ground-rules is that there is no need to 'reinvent the wheel', and that everything should build upon what has gone before. But in creative endeavours there is arguably a need to challenge and question the dominant position. Schools have a subject that could so easily be converted to being the hotbed of innovation and freethinking, but they choose to teach it in the same compartmentalised, specialist fashion that they teach everything else, with objective benchmarks of quality that must be met. Sir Ken Robinson's popular TED speech on the internet argues that this approach is a hangover from the creation of compulsory schooling itself, which was made in the image of the industrial revolution and required students to be obedient, efficient and proficient in order to work in the factories. Sadly this ideology of specialisms and expertise has become so dominant that any modern day polymath would be considered a 'jack-of-all-trades' instead of a genius like the godfathers of the industrial revolution were in the Lunar Society.

The snail shell has inspired people throughout the history of art. Its proportions are considered to be similar to the Golden Spiral. In reality, whilst snail shells exhibit logarithmic spiral growth, they are at an angle distinctly different from that of the golden spiral.

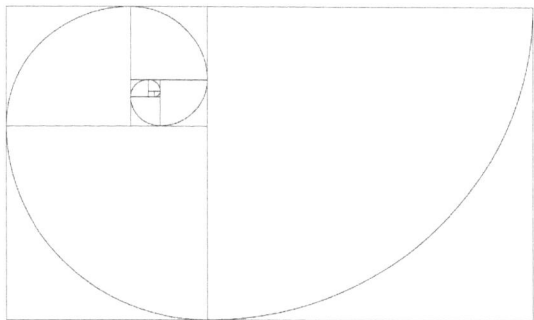

Figure 2 The Golden Spiral

I find all of the mathematical approaches to understanding beauty fascinating. It is intertwined within architecture, Greek philosophy, music, nature and much more. This emphasis upon beauty is a bit alien to me, as I believe that I favour function over form.

Humour me for an instant whilst I give you an example. My grandparents had a long flat tarmac driveway at their bungalow. On the day when the bins were collected, the bin men would simply take the bins that were left at the end of the driveway instead of being left up at the house. This was the 1980's and there were no wheelie bins at this point. Instead, some people simply took their black bin bags and took them down to the end of the driveway for collection. However, there was a problem. Seagulls and foxes would get to the rubbish and it would be strewn across all of the street. The binmen wouldn't take it then either, because it wasn't their job. That would be a street cleaning job I guess. Their union probably did not allow them to clean streets. They were strictly a bin emptying service. My grandfather, who we affectionately called Gugga, decided that he could invent something that meant he could take his solid bin to the end of the driveway, even if it was full and heavy in his old age. He stuck a skateboard underneath it. But that was a little narrow and sometimes meant that the bin was precariously balanced. So he went into the garage and developed the prototype a bit further, by creating a larger base that could match the bottom of the bin, and then four wheels that could spin in all directions as opposed to the locked wheels of the skateboard. His second attempt was still pretty crude, but it worked. And that was only one example of many things that Gugga did to be creative. He didn't wait around for someone to come along with a wheelie bin; he had fashioned one for himself long before hand. I have adopted Gugga's approach of function over form. I am never too concerned about the aesthetics or the 'finish' of a project or a product if it serves its purpose. This really frustrates some people and it even frustrates myself on occasion. I am not much of a perfectionist. I don't perfect the function and then the form. I am primarily interested in the function. I am a pragmatist. I'm happy if it works. If it could work *better*, then I'll continue to work on it. But tidying something up for aesthetic reasons can rub the character off of some projects in my opinion. I like the fact that Gugga's bin wheels did not look like a wheelie bin. The originality and individuality was endearing. It was effective. Why spend more effort when it was going to take rubbish to the end of the driveway?

It is difficult to argue against the pursuit of perfection, as ultimately we all strive to improve our lives, attempting to reach 'completeness' and feeling as if our potential has been fulfilled. In some respects, our whole lives are geared towards improvement. But the paradoxical argument against perfection is that imperfection leads us and motivates us. Without imperfection, there is nothing left to achieve. It is the journey during the constant pursuit of perfection that carries us forward and should it ever be attained, then there is nowhere left to go. Of course, this does not stop some people from trying to get as close to perfection as possible on every occasion that they create something, but even this should be avoided in my opinion. Imperfections are character and eradicating them is eradicating the individuality of a project. I believe there are points when trying to improve something actually goes beyond improvement and is actually counting against the project, forcing it to become bland. Why? Because our ideas of perfection are built on the same mutual assumptions of quality. Advertisers tell us about the perfect bodies and people spend incredible amounts of energy, effort and money trying to achieve these dimensions, sometimes against the unkind will of nature and gravity that ages us all. Even worse, their desire to perfect their image is sometimes at the mercy of their mind. They can be boring. I've met the opposite too; highly intelligent people who should pay a bit more attention to their hygiene! 'Everything in balance' some people will be thinking. Then we must talk about the perfect balance, before we probably concur that perfection is subjective, and my opinion of perfection may not be yours. And if perfection is to be subjective and never complete (in the mathematical sense of no additions or subtractions can be made), then all artistic endeavours must be imperfect.

This argument may seem pedantic and semantic, childishly wasting time on the nature of perfection without reaching any valid point. I apologise. I was building up to that. My point is that people sometimes become creatively paralysed by the concept of perfection. They convince themselves against doing something because 'it won't be any good'. Their creativity becomes stuck in endless tweaks and fiddles in the hope of perfection and they are never satisfied with the outcome if it is anything less than their own expectation of excellence. That is all well and good, if your expectation of excellence is feasible. There are quite a few who expect too much of themselves and can never hope to achieve their goals, at least in one step. They want it all and want it now. They don't want the development or the mistakes. The process of trial and error. They want the result and quickly. Advertisers are great at marketing ways of getting the perfect result quickly, and the result is never perfect. It can't be perfect or you won't buy anything else. Don't get me wrong. I am not a pessimist. I don't believe that we should all give up now and just quit. I believe that we should strive for perfection. But I don't believe we'll all agree upon what we consider to be "perfection". Some will argue it is an equal society and an end to world poverty. Others will argue that it is a society where you can get rich if you want to. Maybe in a perfect world we will all get what we want. I'll settle for a world where we'll all get what we need.

Like many people, the most formative period of my life were my teenage years. I spent four of these years under going orthodentic treatment to straighten my teeth. My nervous childhood had resulted in me being a thumbsucker and it made me goofy. This orthodentic treatment was at best embarrassing, at worst, painful. I feel for every child who has had to undergo the fiddly cleaning process and retweaking sessions, when your teeth all get pressured into another direction. The purpose of this is primarily cosmetic. We all like to have nice teeth. It is on the adverts. People with nice teeth will make good honest politicians and fertile fathers. It is a strange process, whereby we take our youth and recorrect their faces to have a conformist dental record along with everyone else. I wonder what aliens would make of this corrective surgery? Underlying this process is a deeper message to the youth; society rewards people with conformist teeth, and doesn't reward wonky teeth. This is powerful stuff to contend with when you are a teenager in your formative years. You start to think that society may be a bit too shallow and dependent upon appearances. This is particularly harder to deal with if the treatment isn't all that effective, and despite the thumbsucking stopping, the teeth go back to how they were. Then you feel really stuck, because you tried, and failed, to be like everyone else.

Your character is shaped by these events at such a young age. I began to feel incredibly frustrated that image was so important to society. I wanted to study the things that influence our attitudes towards image. I went to college and studied many aspects of media and advertising, deconstructing the images that surround us. It began a fascinating journey that I still haven't finished, but it put me at ease. I realised that the images that surround us aren't real. They are manipulated and altered, nearly always with the goal of making us all feel insecure, so that we would feel better if we bought something. We are sold the image of excellence and perfection, as if a perfect smile will make all the difference. Women are told to be thin, men are told to be more masculine, we are all measured against superhumans that make us feel inadequate. It is just the first step in stripping you of your self esteem so that it can be sold back to you through make up products and technologies that will convince you that you are being really creative. I may have been a thumbsucker, but we all become suckers in the end.

5.1.3. The body:

What can we learn about love, life or creativity from the body of a snail? Their bodies are so different from our own that it becomes difficult to imagine any similarities or possible ways of abstracting metaphors from it. All that is visible of a snail's body is the head and the main body, which supposedly includes one large muscular foot. The rest is a bodily mass, hidden inside the shell that even when crushed, makes little sense. We cannot see the genitals for example, as they are not readily observable to the human eye without magnification.

One thing that is true of snails, and of most other creatures, is that they live in the natural condition. That is, they haven't added technologies to assist or simplify their living. Whereas we are capable of eating with our hands, it is more usual for people to use utensils such as a knife and fork, or maybe chopsticks (some clever people use 'sporks', a spoon with a serrated edge and a fork-like comb edge). These additional utensils are designed to make our lives easier, as are most technologies. Very few of us choose a technology that could make our lives more difficult, despite the fact that some of them do. It takes practice to acclimatise to all technologies (even the knife and fork when we are children, and the chopsticks when we encounter Chinese food). The cumulative effect of all of these technologies renders previous technologies obsolete, and we are sometimes detached from the original sources of technological innovation. For example, the QWERTY keyboard is meant to have evenly spaced the letters of a keyboard so that the typewriter arms didn't collide, which obviously isn't an issue with electronic keyboards. Yet the QWERTY keyboard remains, as we have become accustomed to it. It is not necessary to be an awesome wordsmith anymore either, as the technology can spell and suggest synonyms for you. Just think what you can do with all of the extra space that used to occupy human brains when we had to remember phone numbers and the spelling of everything! However, it seems that our memories are not much better than before, and we should apparently be forced to remember certain things in order to keep our minds sharp. It goes back to the point earlier about imagination; you need to be using it in order for it to work. At the moment that we erase the need to remember anything, do we forget everything? Snails live for years without the additional technologies, so there is an obvious argument for what do we *need* as opposed to *want*? I must admit I do not believe that we should simply exist without the things that bring us happiness, but I do think we should seriously assess the technologies that we surround ourselves with and determine whether they do truly bring us happiness.

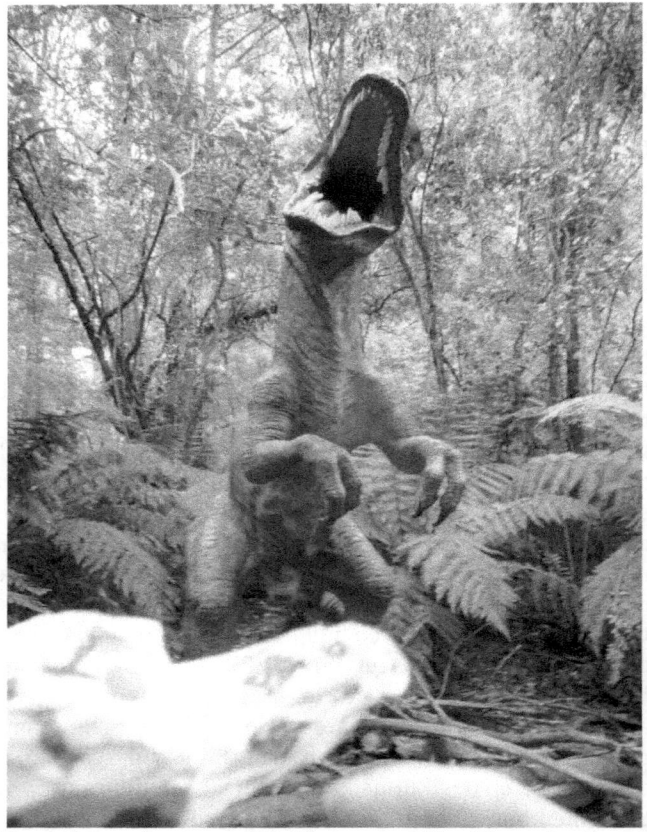

Were things better with dinosaurs? Fruitloop isn't sure

The tentacles upon a snail contain sensory receptors, such as touch and sight. These act the same as our senses, responding to external stimuli and sending impulses to the nervous system. This is where I get confused about biology and wish that I had listened more closely in school, or wish that the teacher would answer my prickly questions. I always assumed that sensory receptors converted external stimuli into something that made 'sense' to the brain; in other words, it had meaning. I've always assumed that this is the basis of consciousness. For example, the nerve endings in my hand detect heat and tell my brain that it is hot. Because of the human faculties of consciousness and memory, I don't put my hand on it, because I remember that being burned is painful. These two elements combined are a defence mechanism. Now, if a snail can 'sense' heat or some other threat, what process is telling it to retract the tentacle or go even further into the shell? Of course, it's their memory:

> *While the Aplysia snail, common to marine waters off California, has 20,000 neurons in its central nervous system, compared to about 1 trillion for a human, the UCLA scientists say the gastropods are similar to people in how they learn and form memories. For the study, Glanzman's team first applied electric shocks to the snails, then gently prodded an organ in their mid-section. The snails responded by contracting for 50 seconds. A week later, the scientists touched the snails in the same spot, and again the creatures contracted -- this time for at least 30 seconds. For the scientists, that was evidence the mollusks had formed a negative memory to being shocked and prodded. The research team then injected the snails with a compound that blocked the action of an enzyme called PKM, which is associated with memory. When they poked the snails 24 hours later, the creatures barely moved, suggesting the bad memory of being poked had been dulled.[4]*

Now, this seems hideously obvious when I read and think about it, but it rarely goes through my mind when I see a snail on the floor. There will no doubt be some animal lovers, who are slapping their

---

[4] **Snail memory study offers hope to trauma victims.** By Alex Dobuzinskis. Edited by Julie Steenhuysen, Steve Gorman and Peter Bohan.
  http://www.reuters.com/article/2011/04/26/us-memory-snails-idUSTRE73P7R920110426 (Accessed on 31st August 2012)

foreheads at my stupidity right now, but I must warn that you are in the minority of people who actually think about a snail's memory. And don't think that I will join your minority, because I will most likely forget. The sad probability is that our ability for abstract thought doesn't really see the world from the perspective of a snail that much. Perhaps we should. If we considered how others felt and used our ability to empathise more often, we may live in a nicer world. If we go back to the shell briefly, the snail doesn't need it to protect them from other snails but from predators. It is not an impenetrable defence. I find it a shame that humans supposedly have the intellect to lead the food chain yet we attack one another too. Imperial countries ludicrously defend through attack. We say we are defending our principles (like democracy), or ourselves (from terrorism) whereas we are defending our privileged positions. We live in an unequal society and it seems that we cannot sustain our lifestyles if we are to live equitably with one another, so we need to suppress others to do so. Like snails, humans can be crushed. Not within the natural hierarchy of the food chain, but a hierarchy developed by constructed means. We find it difficult to relate to the pictures of poverty upon our televisions because they are too abstract. For a start, they are on our television, which is a piece of technology that not every one in the world can afford. Secondly, it is so hard to imagine ourselves without our basic needs, like a flushing toilet. Imagine we had to swap with an impoverished human for a day. What would we make of their life? What would they make of ours? Would we change our own lives when we returned to our own homes? The likelihood is that you'd appreciate what you've got a bit more, but would you forsake any of it? I'm not suggesting for any second that I am forsaking anything. I'm as guilty as the next person of indulging myself in all that our society has to offer, even if it is constructed at the expense of someone else. It isn't easy to live by an altruistic belief system, especially as it seems so pointless when there is no critical mass of people acting simultaneously to help. And there isn't the political will to cancel the odious debt within developing nations when we can use it to get natural resources cheaply, at least not in the same way that the politicians bailed out the banking system from it's corporate debt. That said, politicians would argue that they are elected to act in the electorates' interest, not the global interest, and they would be right. It is when they act in their own interest that it is annoying.

56

Like the body of snails, they are slimy and change shape to suit the terrain, or popular opinion. Few carry a bona fide set of principles that govern their direction. Like snails they probe the public opinion before slowly moving forward in the direction of the most votes. This is great if you believe in the wisdom of the crowd, but our collective wisdom is only as good as the information we receive and choose to interpret. I won't regurgitate my media studies A-Level here, I feel as if I have darkened the tone too much and showered my champagne socialism over the whole project. I apologise.

The bodies of snails are also soft and slimy, which directly inspired me to make papier-mâché versions of them with my bank statements. Let's take a look at some more pictures before exploring the behaviour of a snail.

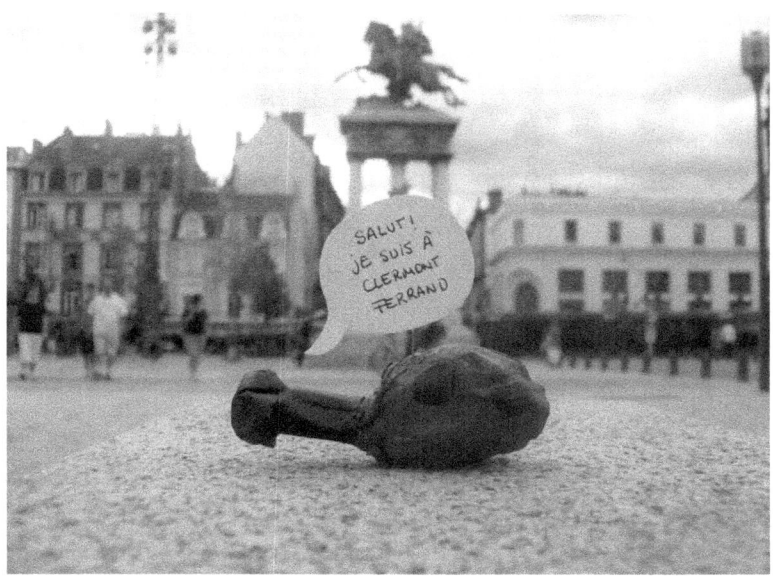

Lily in Clermont Ferrand, France

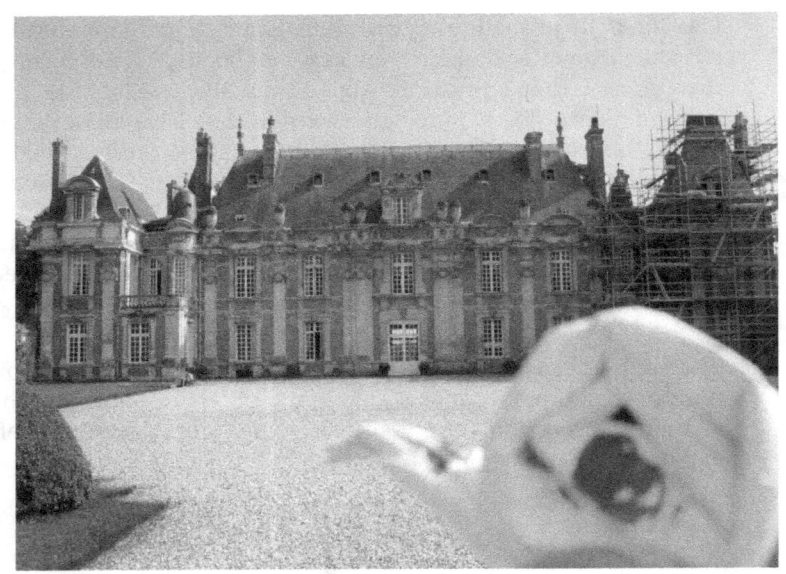

Elsewhere in France: Klok at the Château de Miromesnil

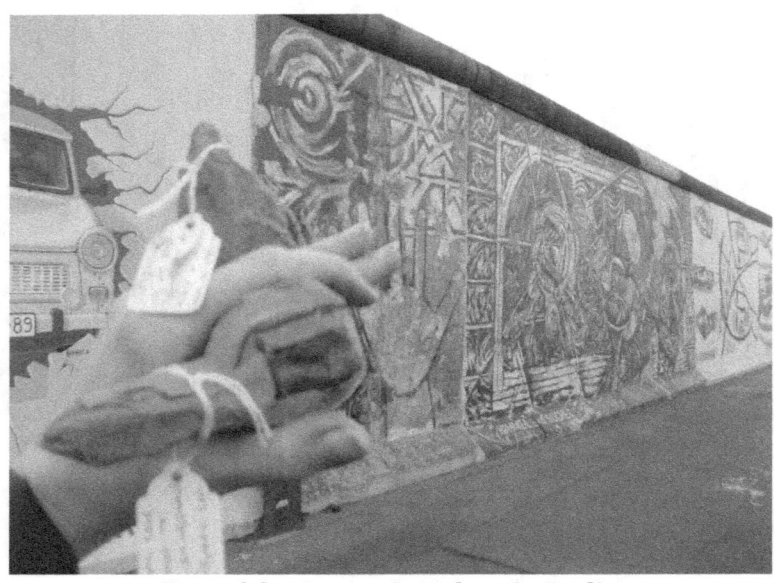

Two of the Canary Squadron in Berlin

5.2 The behaviour of a snail:

5.2.1. Speed:

Snails are notoriously slow. We use the analogy of a 'snail's pace' when describing somebody who is moving slowly. Because there are no fast moving limbs for us to witness, it is difficult to imagine how they are moving at all. It is not until we are on the other side of a transparent surface whilst they crawl across it that we can see their muscular movement propelling them forward. What can we learn about love, life or creativity from this speed?

Most obviously, in life, we could perhaps appreciate the slower lifestyle. We have grown so accustomed to everything being instant that the idea of waiting for anything seems abhorrent. It is difficult to identify a pleasure in waiting, but I think we can all remember the pleasure in a wait finally being over, which cannot happen without the wait! Everything, all of the time, arguably leads to excess and the rapid interaction with food, culture and information means that perhaps we are valuing it less. If we learnt to spend time and savour these occasions, perhaps we would be happier and more appreciative people. I guess it depends on your opinion. It is possible to observe the speed of a snail and be thankful that our lives are faster, and that we've pursued a societal policy of eliminating waiting wherever possible. In the world of atoms, we are ruled by the production triangle, but in the world of bits even that paradigm seems uncertain.

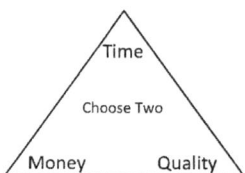

Figure 3 The Production Triangle paradigm

In the old paradigm, you could have any two sides of the triangle but you couldn't have all three. If you wanted something of good quality quickly, you would have to pay for it. If you wanted something good quality cheaply, you would have to wait for it. If you wanted something cheap and quickly, it probably wasn't very good quality. This is still the case to a large extent within the physical world of atoms. If you wish to board a plane before everyone else you pay a bit more for priority boarding. If you want express shipping on your internet purchase, you pay a bit more. This is because 'snail mail' means we have to wait longer, and if we've got a bit of extra cash in our pocket, we don't have to wait. Of all the finite resources on this earth that humans can understand and are terrified of, it is our own personal time. We know we won't live forever. At some stage death will come along and we want to feel as if we have given the 'living' bit a bloody good go before we leave the planet. Therefore, if something is wasting our time, we get pretty annoyed about it. Admittedly, not many people get angry with a delayed train because we feel like we will die soon. We get angry because it is an inconvenience, and an unexpected one at that. We made a plan for our time and the slow train is messing with that plan. You were going to meet your friend at the shopping mall but the train is late. You were going to get a session at the gym but the traffic is bad. All of this stress comes from our expectations of the future not matching our current situation. As Nicholas Nassim Taleb expresses in his book Black Swans, you only 'miss' the train if you were expecting to 'catch' it. If you simply arrived with no preconceived ideas of when trains were leaving, you'd be in a happier space. You may be upset to discover that you have to wait for ages for the next one, but it is better waiting in a happier mood than fuming in a bad mood about something that hasn't happened. I commute a lot on trains, and occasionally I lose myself and get angry at the service. But mostly I have learnt to deal with the unpredictability, and find pleasure in the moments where I have to wait, because it means I have a legitimate reason to indulge myself in reading. In the world of digital bits, it is often possible to have quality, for free, whenever you want it. I believe it is this inversion of the production triangle that leaks into our everyday world and affects our perception of reality, whereby things are rarely 'instant' in the real world. Text messages and status updates are common distractions in the queue for what used to be called 'fast' food (it's cheap and quick... but is it any good?).

60

Our perception of life is warped by the idea that we could have it all so much better/quicker/cheaper online. Shops, cinemas and concerts all pay close attention to the 'experience' as it is their only advantage over the vapidity of your computer screen. It is as if the marketplace is asking you to go snail-like, as if there is more to gain from the buying process than simply the consumption of goods alone. Go slow, enjoy yourself and get your monies worth! It is a weird bastardisation of the production triangle whereby the quality is now in spending the time and the money as part of a shopping 'experience', instead of the homogenous click-of-a-button that you use to buy your cabbage and watch your porn.

The Christian group 'True Love Waits' believe in sexual purity until you've found the partner that you want to be with, and the abstinence is meant to last until both parties have entered into a biblical marriage. Unfortunately, as I came from the 'try before you buy' school of thought, I cannot really comment on whether the belief is a powerful one. Critics argue that a majority of people who take the 'True Love Waits' pledge actually break it, but I'm pretty sure that those who keep it detract some meaning and purpose from it. Aside from the obvious advantages of knowing that your partner is sexually 'pure', there must be some excitement that the two lovers will embark on a journey of sexual discovery together, as opposed to the slightly more chaotic and haphazard nature of dating shenanigans whereby sexual etiquette is a bit more subjective; "If I sleep with him/her on the first date will they think I am loose?" The desire to satisfy lust is often greater than the quest to find love, and therefore the waiting seems eternal, especially for the curious. I hate to admit it, but I think this is probably an area where there is a genuine generational difference in society. Without sounding old, I remember that my sexual curiosity was fuelled by a mystique surrounding sex that was only ever alluded to in uncomfortable school lessons or gleaned from whatever print pornography I could find. Books like the Karma Sutra or the Joy of Sex were giggly bibles where I learnt that I had to have facial hair before I could have intercourse. Contemporary adolescents can find all kinds of sexual pornography in abundance on a variety of platforms, to the point where there is probably no mystique attached to it whatsoever. They are probably exposed to explicit imagery at a younger age and with greater ease than we care to imagine. I don't know whether the net effect is that there is no longer a race to sexuality when it is so abundant and un-mystical, or whether this exposure is an accelerant. But I do believe in the pervasive power of media to influence, and the portrayal within pornography is no doubt influencing a generation of people as to what is expected of them in the bedroom. This is a horrifying thought, as there is little about unity or respect within pornography; it is all about instant gratification. If we build our perception of sexual relationships up around this constructed imagery, we are once again not prepared for the reality of life. People bounce from relationship to relationship on the basis that it isn't what they were expecting. Instead of critically reflecting upon their expectations, they are just moving on to repeat the disaster until reality bites and some wisdom kicks in (usually about nine sexual partners later for men, four for women, according to one report[5]). This process of trial and error in relationships is arguably not a bad thing, as it acts as a sort of 'positioning' experience whereby you learn what you do and don't want in a relationship. But this is only the case if there is some critical reflection taking place, and it doesn't work if you simply repeat the same errors. It is not unusual for people to identify the flaws in their partners but not in themselves; such is the stupid nature of the human beast. I don't want to pass judgement on whether abstinence or promiscuity is the best way forward, but I believe that the speed of a snail can teach us to slow down and truly experience sex as opposed to hurrying in the belief that a 'quickie' is a kite-mark for true lust.

As a child I witnessed my parents' divorce, and I subsequently have a dualistic sentiment about relationships. On the one hand, I think that my parents should have persevered through the hard times and stuck with the marriage. Here I would like to evoke the image of a snail moving slowly through time, crossing whatever terrain it comes across, up or down, and sticking to whatever nature brings its way. On the other hand I believe that the individuals have to answer to themselves. I don't respect stories of stoic perseverance for the sake of the institutional value of marriage, and I completely understand how individuals, when confronted with a finite period

---

[5]http://www.telegraph.co.uk/women/sex/sexual-health-and-advice/8958520/Average-man-has-9-sexual-partners-in-lifetime-women-have-4.html (Accessed 9th October 2012)

of time on this planet, feel pressure to pursue happiness in whatever way they can. I don't believe there is a prize in the afterlife for devotion to God or to anyone else. Here I would simply like to evoke the image of a snail. I have never seen one with a ring on its non-existent finger, and I've never seen one with a load of tin cans tied to its asshole as it happily slides off on a honeymoon. They are individuals. Whilst nature provides us with plenty of examples of creature companionship (read a book on penguins if you like that sort of thing), I believe that humans are only interested in relationships with others because of the advantages that it offers the individual self. Put simply, some people don't want to be alone, in life or death. Others do, which is a more explicit example of individualism. There are some spectacular exceptions, and these are exceptions that warm my heart. In some exceptional cases, carers can be selfless people who stick with their sick family or friends through adversity and rarely put themselves first, especially not to the extent that they would abandon their dependant for the sake of an easy life. But even in these cases, they are occasionally held in by the centrifugal force of guilt, and the idea that abandonment would haunt any pursuit of an easy life anyway. 'I could never leave them' is not a statement about 'them'; it is a statement about 'I'. The exceptional cases are when somebody has identified a sick person's needs and subsequently devotes chunks of their own life to delivering them, not because of some imagined social contract, but purely out of the belief that it is a necessity and someone must do it. Whilst these extraordinary circumstances of care and kindness should be benchmarks for human civilisation, they are not unique to humans. Vampire bats regurgitate blood to help sick bats recover, dogs are known to adopt all kinds of animal orphans and dolphins apparently do numerous acts of kindness for other species too, like saving surfers from sharks and helping whales from being beached. This kind of caring doesn't even fit the notion that we protect our own species to assure our collective survival. Cynical individualists can get lost because dogs and dolphins are proof that some creatures are nice to others just for the sake of it.

I've digressed again. What can the speed of a snail teach us about creativity? Well, I personally enjoy creating things rapidly and under pressure, forcing instinct to leave an impression on any creation. I think it makes for a more interesting analysis of art when we consider that it comes from the gut or the deep recesses of the brain instead of a contemplative, thoughtful place. I have experienced paralysis through analysis so I favour momentum. I hate making mistakes, and I cringe at some of the mistakes that I have made, but I believe that it is impossible to achieve perfection so the mistakes are the character of some art on occasion. I personally prefer the prolific filmmakers and musicians who make some questionable art to the ones who offer occasional gems with ten years in between. That said, whilst I like to make a lot of things and often, I actually view it with a much longer-term goal in mind. My theory is that I *am* going slowly; everything I have made so far is just the beginning of a much longer journey where I hope to mature and develop, sustaining creativity as I go along. I may be quick in the short term, but it's all part of a much slower process. A snail is actually moving slowly by making lots of muscles move in a rapid wavelike motion.

We actually consume other people's creativity very quickly; with so much culture around, must of us don't spend too long actually concentrating on any one thing at all. For creative people, this speed of consumption is a bit of a shame. In the past, I would invest in the hideously overpriced compact disc of my favourite bands and then listen to the music religiously, desperate to get my monies worth. The net result was an appreciation of the music that I rarely achieve today. I would listen to all the songs and know them inside out, whereas now that only happens for a handful of my favourite artists. Indeed, some musicians have stopped preparing albums altogether, as they are rarely consumed as such. Some artists take years to gain recognition for the labour that they put into their craft; others are desperate to get recognition as quickly as possible. Fame at any cost. Andy Warhol spoke of a future where everyone will be world famous for fifteen minutes. The idea that anyone can gain notoriety without any particular talent is no longer that strange, we are surrounded in media by celebrities who have achieved this. The vapidity of their fame is characterised by the fact that they lack any real consistency of talent, and their rapid rise is matched by a rapid fall. Anyone who is indulging in creative past-times in the hope that they will become famous would do well to explore Malcolm Gladwell's book Outliers, which talked of the 10,000 hours needed to become 'expert' at something. Even when Marshall McLuhan feted the

Beatles as being the amateurs that challenged the ground-rules of popular music experts, he failed to take into account their hours of gigs in Hamburg before they hit the 'big time'. It is believed that getting good at something takes time. This isn't a contradiction of my earlier assertion that pursuit of perfection can be fruitless. Time spent engaging with something isn't necessarily time spent in the pursuit of perfection. You could spend hours making music, from concept through to completion via recording and performance. Or you could spend hours learning how to riff through the keys as quickly as possible. The riffing is great, but if you cannot marry this skill into music in a larger context, then it is kind of pointless. It is a circus trick. A musical masturbation. It bears little fruit. I'm suggesting that the speed of a snail can teach us to put time into our creative endeavours, but I'm not suggesting that we get hung up on them without seeing the bigger picture. That said; nothing is a waste of time if you enjoy the time you waste. Go fast or slow, just be happy[6].

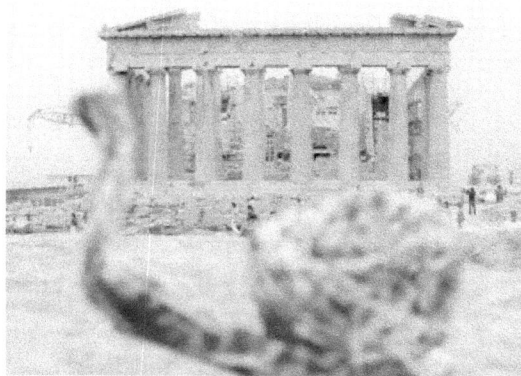

Speedy in Athens, Greece

---

[6] Let me change the subject for a moment. I had a teacher whose wife was once cycling to work and rode up along side a heavy goods vehicle. The lorry driver did not see the woman in his mirrors and as he turned into a side street, she fell under the giant wheels of the vehicle. Her head popped like the fragile snail shell as the weight of the vehicle went over her skull. She actually survived, but her life was never the same again. I'm only mentioning this because I believe that strange things happen in life, and we should never forget that.

5.2.2. Lifestyle:

Obviously I'm not talking about their hobbies or the way they decorate their home. I'm talking about their diet, sexuality and sleeping habits.

5.2.2.1. Diet:

Snails are fond of beer, so much so that gardeners set 'beer traps' to lure them in and drown them. It seems that humans aren't the only species to drink themselves to death. What can this teach us about life? That drink is fine in moderation I guess. The same goes for salt. Snails cannot tolerate salt because of osmosis, which sees the snail's internal water content pass through the semi-permanent membrane of the snail's skin to try and balance the salt content on the outside. This makes the snail seemingly melt. Whilst this doesn't happen to humans, it is worth noting that both salt and beer can screw up a human body when consumed in excess. It seems pointless labouring the analogy. Perhaps more interestingly in the human situation, is why do we like to consume alcohol? Neuroscientists believe that we drink to reduce thought associations in our mind. The alcohol includes ethanol, which damages the communication between neurons so much so that electrical signals are not sent as normal and associations between ideas do not emerge as readily. These associations are how we make sense of the world, which is a continuous burden that we could do without. With alcohol we start living less in our heads, and more in the here and now. It's a form of transcendence that others may seek in religion. Social anthropologists argue that we drink to break the taboos that govern society, and that it is our collective perception of what alcohol does that means we can behave badly, as if 'being drunk' lets us get away with bad behaviour. Either way. I'm guessing these aren't the same concerns of snails. Can we confront our pressures without relying on alcohol? Many people would argue 'yes'. It is difficult to find whether there are teetotal snails, but there are certainly humans who choose not to drink booze. If I am to take life lessons from snails, beer is fine as long as I do it in moderation.

I'm being too detached. Let me reflect more honestly for a moment. Why do I drink? Well, usually I do it socially. There is usually a crowd around and we are all drinking. I associate it with relaxing. I believe I am more relaxed if I drink. Like some others, I occasionally drink at home by myself to relax after work. This is meant to be shameful but I believe it is more common than many realise. Ironically, the effects of drink actually stress me out more than relax me. I tend to drink to relieve stress but it is only a fleeting experience. I am awful with a hangover, and drift into a deep sense of self-loathing around the edge of sleep, as I wake up. I always imagine that I will have a far more sober future, and I have done large periods of time with no drink on multiple occasions. Thankfully I have developed a bit more of a sensibility about drink as I have got older, because in my youth I would have simply ramped up the alcohol intake and gone for the 'hair of the dog'. The crash after these binges would be awful, but I was constantly fascinated by the self-destruction of it all. This sounds ludicrous, but I enjoy pushing the limit within most of the things that I do, so drinking was just an extension of that. I believe that 'you have to go there to come back'. I respect empathy over sympathy. Drinking has led me to moments of extreme absences of inhibition, most of which are cringe-worthy, but some of which have majorly impacted positively upon the course of my life. I've worked on projects that began with drunken conversations and I've had relationships that began with drunken conversations; I don't regret any of those. Was alcohol essential to either? Probably not, but it was still present.

Continental Europeans generally don't understand the binge-culture upon the British Isles and there are multiple theories put forward to suggest why it exists. I won't go into it here, but I find it fascinating how society supposedly impacts upon individual behaviour. I've already mentioned that I usually drink on social occasions and I doubt I would drink if it weren't socially acceptable. It's interesting how many smokers cite peer pressure or the desire to look cool in front of others when they talk about the reason for starting. We are social creatures, linked through friendships and relationships that influence our behaviour. I have no idea whether snails have the same pressures. The snails that I have kept in a glass tank to complete these observations don't seem to have any relationship to one another, they all seem to act autonomously. This is an important observation. How much of our life is based around interactions with others? Almost all of it. The majority of us make money as a result of providing some kind of service or product for others to consume. Imagine we were all just looking after ourselves. Most of our identity is built around the way that we interact with other people. According to a bit of casual research, snails don't really communicate with one another other than to mate, or to hunt (in the case of the carnivorous snails[7]). So there is very little social connection between snails apart from the mating, which is a strange process indeed.

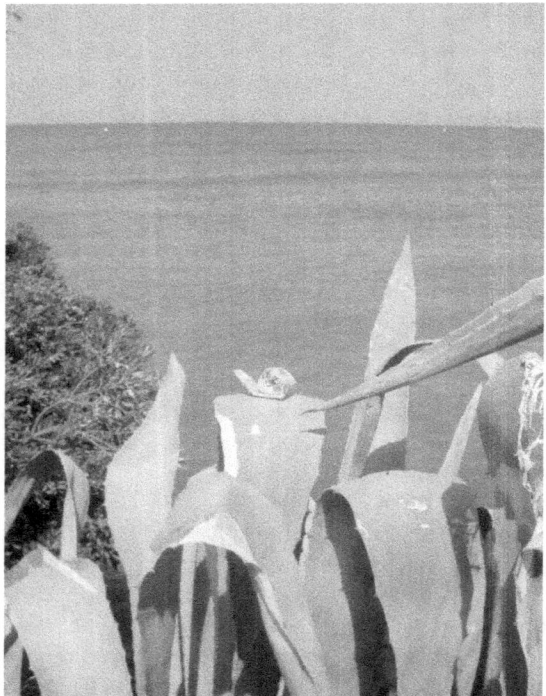

Seila in Crete

---

[7] Yes, carnivorous ones. Forget the beer; let's briefly talk about the food. I fed my snails lettuce, tomatoes and cucumber. I also put eggshells in to provide calcium for their shells, but cuttlefish bone is usually best for this. Most land snails are herbivores but some breeds of snail like to eat other snails and slugs. Any vegetarians who hoped that I would be inspired by the herbivore ways of a snail are probably disappointed.

5.2.2.2. Sexuality:

Most land snails are hermaphrodites, carrying both the sexual organs of the male and female. Water snails have separate sexes but we're not discussing them here, so I only share this information to demonstrate the extent of my pub-quiz trivia knowledge. Unfortunately, this is the limit of my knowledge, as I cannot say why land snails need to mate when they carry all the necessary equipment to do it to themselves. But they do.

There is quite a bit of foreplay preceding snail sex. Two snails caress each other with their tentacles, nibble at lips, and rock their bodies back and forth. It goes on for hours before mating commences. I cannot determine whether this is the equivalent of minutes in human speed, because snails move slowly, or whether they are genuinely good at foreplay. At this point, men are rolling their eyes: "Snails can teach us to spend longer at foreplay". Think want you will gentlemen. I'm just stating the facts. This is when the kinky shit starts for some snail species, because to signal they're ready to mate, each pierces the body of the other with a long, sharp spear, called a 'love dart'. Apparently, it sexually stimulates them.

Snail sex involves two mates aligning their bodies so the penis of each is inserted into the vagina of the other. This also goes on for hours. The snails exchange sperm; then each stores this sperm in a special storage pouch and uses it to fertilize their own eggs, sometimes over the course of several months. The majority of the sperm that they'll share are internally digested before reaching the storage pouch.[8] This obviously impacts on the fertility success rate. Therefore nature has provided the 'love dart', which transfers mucus that prevents a snail's body from digesting so much semen. How chivalrous. However, most snails don't see too well, so one-third of 'love darts' miss their target (or fail to penetrate.) Do the snails seem to mind being harpooned? Yes, actually, they do. There's research indicating that snails frequently jostle in an effort to stab, but not be stabbed.

Snails lay their eggs singly or in clusters of dozens, depending on

---

[8] I said "digested". The majority of snail sperm is digested. If you get this right in a pub quiz you'll either a) look really clever or b) receive strange looks. Either way, you're drinking in the wrong kind of pub if this question comes up.

the species. Some bury their eggs in soft, moist soil or hide them in moist, protected places like leaf litter and under logs. The eggs hatch in about two to four weeks, depending on the species and favorable weather (they wait to hatch until conditions are right.) As soon as they hatch, the baby snails begin feeding on their own eggshell, as it is rich in calcium. Greedy snails may also consume any other shells they find, even if the egg is still occupied and un-hatched. At this stage, the tiny snails are transparent. In about three months they'll look like the snails they we recognise, but it will be a further two or three years before they reach adult size and sexual maturity, and this is towards the end of their life in the wild, although it is believed that captive snails have lived as long as 10 or 15 years. Their life span depends on the species and most snails don't make it through their first year because of predators.

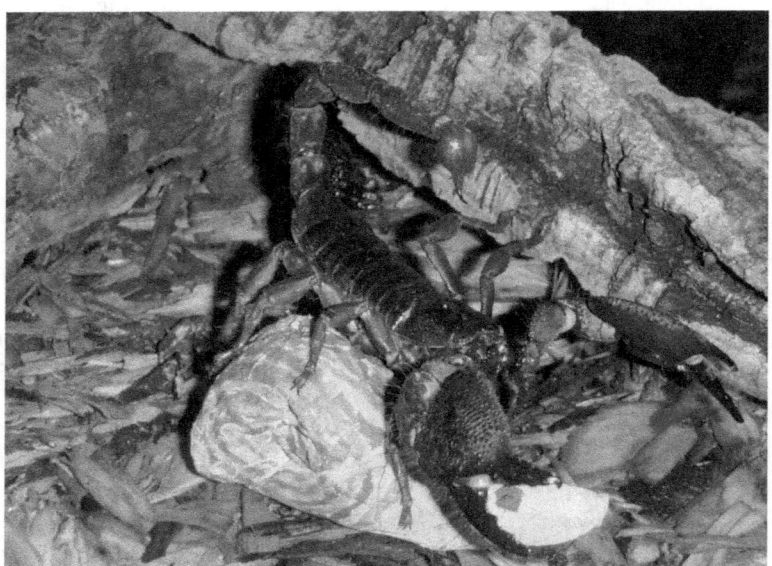

Daisy with a scorpion in Animalarium in Borth, Wales

What can any of this process tell us about life? Well, one can assume that the land snails have got a lot more empathy for one another, as they know how the other snail feels. Humans have the misfortune of being two separate sexes and each individual requires the opposite sex to reproduce. There is a whole pile of cultural artifacts dedicated to either men or females who are keen to understand the opposite sex. Ultimately understanding one another is impossible; even people who are capable of imagining someone else's perspective cannot truly begin to imagine everything that happen as a result of our bodies. Think about our relationship to our own body. We know our own genitals, nipples and body hair better than others. Whilst we may share our body with others on occasion, we have spent everyday of our lives with it! Our bodies play a major part on the way that we are perceived in society. The colour of your skin or the size of your hips can have an impact upon the way people treat you. I had (and continue) to have ginger hair. It was a source of some ridicule at school, now I tend to hear from some women how much they envy my hair colour (no man has ever said this to me). I'm fairly certain that some girlfriends were surprised to find that my pubic hair was ginger too, despite it being logical. Now, this ginger hair, and the way that I have responded to the reactions to it, has had an impact upon how I behave in a group of people. Add another variable: my teeth. And another: my height. Another: my nose. The list goes on for everybody, and it formulates a complex character around our physicality. The media would have us believe that some sexy women lament that guys never ask them out, presumably because of physical intimidation or just lack of self-confidence. I don't believe this for an instant, as I know there are plenty of dickhead males that believe in their own good looks and have the confidence to make sure everyone else is aware too. What these beautiful women probably mean is they never get 'nice' guys asking them out. This is because the mythical 'nice' guy is tremendously difficult to come across. Nearly all men have tried being the 'nice' guy at some point in their teenage years; befriending girls in the hope that they will one day fall in love. The net effect of this is: 'I like you as a friend'. Sucker! People assume that our own body is the physical representation of our inner self, as if beautiful people are nice and fat or ugly people are lazy or stupid. This is ludicrous, but it is surprising how many people are guilty of making these assumptions. Whilst teaching in university I've had people assume I am a student because of my dress sense and boyish good looks (!). Cumulatively, each of these interactions and experiences add up and contribute to our whole character. We cannot completely understand what it is to be someone else, man or woman.

Yet we must find someone if we are to reproduce, and part of that process is feeling emotionally and/or physically attracted to someone else, which is a platform for sexual arousal. The idea that snails play together first is quite sweet, albeit that it results in a stabbing of sorts[9]. I'm not going to go into what this foreplay could possibly mean for love, life or creativity. The obvious association is that foreplay is essential to love (and therefore life) and we should be creative in our discovery of one another's bodies. But that is bullshit, because sex, and sexuality is such a personal subject for every individual that the idea that there can be some over-arching prescription for how to approach it denies the beautifully complex nature of sex and sexuality. It is our fascination with the subject that sells countless magazines proclaiming to teach 'how to drive her wild' or 'make him love you forever'. These articles are fuelling the problem of expectation. Far from educating our lovers on the topic of sex or sexuality, they present an exaggerated 'normality', which acts as a benchmark for people to compare themselves to. This is a dangerous territory; what can and cannot happen within your sexual partnerships is completely dependent on trust and the strength of the relationship. Reading an article about what to do in the bedroom is only warping expectations. Don't get me wrong; I'm not being prudish about the articles. I think they are fun and I hope most readers interpret them as such. Whilst an article that says 'how to make her come over and over again' would be fun to read, it isn't taking into account the awkwardness (and painfulness, presumably) of a persistent masturbator who has referred to a magazine for love tips. That's right. Your sexual partner isn't a vehicle that has a user manual that can instruct you in these matters. You become more confident at sex with your partner the longer you spend together exploring one another sexually.

---

[9] I'm resisting the urge to write 'pork sword' in the body of the text, but I'm giggling so profusely at the words that I feel 'pork sword' should appear in the footnotes.

5.2.2.3. Habitat:

Snails like to live in moist and dark places, such as marshes, woodlands, pond margins and gardens. They hide under leaves, rocks, under flower-pots and amongst the other junk that you keep in your garden. Snails don't tend to travel too far, but they can easily be affected by disturbances in their environment, and because they're unable to move quickly they may not escape a dangerous change. Mostly snails are dispersed by water carrying them, like flooding and down streams of rain or river water. Humans also disperse them in soil or in pots of flowers purchased at a garden center. Some have been found attached to the fur of an animal, which is a good way of hitching a ride. There are also claims that tiny snail eggs can be picked up and dispersed by wind. There are some snails who live in warmer regions and estivate when weather conditions are dry. Estivation is like hibernation as it is a reduced state of metabolic activity, but the sleep isn't as deep as hibernation. These snails bury themselves, withdrawing into their shell and plugging the opening to conserve moisture. The snails stay that way until it rains. When it does, they must eat, mate and lay eggs before the environment dries up again! As the majority of snails tend to enjoy dark, moist spaces, they enjoy the rain and they enjoy the night. They especially enjoy a rainy night. I cannot ascertain whether they like rainy nights because humans don't like them, therefore reducing the potential for being crushed. I think this is purely coincidental. They also like to be close to vegetation, as this is their source of food. What can this teach us about our own lives?

Humans usually sleep at night, because we require the daylight to see and do things. However, the birth of controllable light (fire torches or lamps) meant we could begin to spend time deliberately awake in the dark. Now, with electricity, many people are awake throughout the night either working or playing. I prefer working at night because I don't get interrupted the same ways that I do in the daytime. I can develop a deeper concentration than I would normally do when emails and phone calls come in. However, this has become less successful as my work becomes more international and emails are coming in from all different time zones. If I am to succeed creatively at night, I must switch off all the apparatus that can cause an unexpected distraction, especially internet and telephones. Music can stay as long as it is not too distracting. With the distractions gone, I can work quite successfully. Ironically, I could probably work quite well in this way in the daytime too, but part of the contemporary approach to work is that you must be contactable at all times. Personally I think this is quite unproductive. I find it strange that electricity should have freed humans from the burden of physical work, yet it seems to have tied us up inextricably to lots of brainwork. I often wonder how people went through the effort of handwriting letters, walking to a post-box and sending them by 'snail mail'. I know I wouldn't receive nearly as much email if the sender had to go through the same rigmarole as sending 'snail mail'. Email is so easy to send that it has become an overwhelmingly inefficient process of communication too, because I am now more stressed at checking my inbox than I am at checking my post-box. I know what is in the post-box. It's bills. My email is going to have messages asking me to *do* things, as well as *pay* things. This is far more daunting. And the sheer volume of email (most of which is trivial) makes reading through it laborious. I'm guessing that snails prefer the night because many of their predators are not nocturnal, so it is better for survival. Similarly, I prefer the night to get things done without anyone trying to contact me.

What can the nocturnal lifestyle teach us about love? We associate the night with love a lot more than the day. We spend so much of our day at work that the night is when we often see our loved ones. The majority of sexual intercourse that takes place in the world most likely happens in the local night-time; then followed by sleeping in close proximity with the partner. I'm not sure whether this improves conception or whether it is just practical given our daily routines. We should probably judge potential partners in the cold light of day but we often socialise with alcohol in low light conditions to soften the harsh blows of reality! It is sad that most people don't often get to spend so many days with their partners; working five sevenths of the week. That said; I know people that wouldn't manage much more proximity and cherish work because it lets them get out of the house. Are we meant to spend more time with our partners? Relationships can survive when the only time that is spent together is evenings, weekends and the occasional holiday. Some people are more independent than others, and I think it is important to communicate your needs to your partner early on to avoid them feeling either lonely or smothered. It is meeting the demands of others that can make relationships so difficult and complex, because a person's needs could change. I've had the confusing situation whereby the thing that one woman loved me for became a similar reason as to why we broke up, albeit with a different title. Here's a table that explains some of this predicament:

The reason they fell in love:	The reason they are breaking up:
You are ambitious.	You work too hard.
You are funny.	You don't take any thing seriously.
You are good looking.	You are vain.
You are independent.	You are selfish.

These aren't strict opposites, but they are connected, and when someone's perspective changes one can quickly become the other. It is difficult because the assumption is that the same person comes home every night, but the likelihood is that we haven't shared a great deal of one another's experiences, and these experiences change us. Yes, you can share an edited version of the daily events once you get home in the form of a recollected narrative. Depending on your partner's storytelling skills and the drama of the event, this can either be riveting or so boring you want to bury them in the garden. Or, you don't share the things that are having an effect on your thinking, and one day you look at your lover and either you or they realise that you've 'grown apart'. This is a strange expression, but I imagine it to be like a plant that has separated and is growing in a different direction from the rest of the plant, and plants grow towards light. When we find the person we want to be with we say 'we want to spend the rest of our days with them', which we've already established is not likely to be the case, at least before retirement. My point is that we live predominantly in the day yet we sell this time to an employer. We give our loved ones the off-cuts of our time. Whilst snails come out at night to eat and breed, we eat and breed at night because we are too busy in the day. Of course, we need to work, despite the fact that most of us are involved in jobs that have been constructed for employment and have no true need. Traffic wardens must collect revenues from people who park a piece of technology irresponsibly, probably abandoned by a person who needed to get somewhere equally unnecessary in the grand scheme of the universe. Jobs are important because we make them important, in the same way that religion used to be important. It is the universal paradigm that work is necessary, despite the fact that eating, sleeping and reproducing are probably the only necessary elements for our survival. The fact that sleep is free means most cave-people were searching for food and someone to reproduce with; such is the cave-person's life. Now we've convoluted our society to such an extent that many people don't find time to eat properly and many have rubbish relationships! I'm generalising of course, and probably projecting my own experience as opposed to a universal experience. Some people will be thinking; 'I eat well and have a healthy relationship!' Good for you. You should probably write this book because you obviously have the whole thing worked out. If you are free of any materialism, any status anxiety, any work related stress, I applaud you. I applaud you because you have achieved this in a society that has inadvertently created constructs that are diametrically opposed to this way of living, most notably businesses in the pursuit of profits. If you manage to eat well it is because either you can afford to grow your own (with the time and space) or you can afford to buy it (with money). Many people cannot afford good food because they have no access to either the space or the money, and need the time to work for money in order to get the space. Making a relationship work doesn't necessarily require the time or the money (prostitution aside). I don't know what constitutes a successful relationship and I'm concluding that I cannot find it in observing snails. They are such individual creatures that only require another snail for the sake of reproduction. If I was to take this point and map it to human relationships I think I would struggle to find a girlfriend.

5.2.2.4. Ability to stick to surfaces:

Snails can climb walls and even hang upside down with the adhesive qualities of their mucus. What would this change in perspective do for us? I think a good example is the fascination when flying in planes or looking from high buildings, temporarily viewing the world we live in differently. Creatively, this change in perspective can inspire us to think differently. Looking over a city from a tall building means that I can appreciate the geography far more than I can on the ground. For example, I was once stood in Canary Wharf in London. From the floor on which I stood it was obvious that London sat in the Thames Valley river basin, with the Chiltern Hills to the north and the North Downs to the south (just to be confusing). This is obvious when considering history or geography lessons in school where civilisations gathered around water, and their cities pointed out on a map. Maps are different perspectives, human constructs that are different from the primacy of our immediate senses. Standing in the tall building or taking off in the plane, I can *see* the landscape. This momentary, godlike perspective fulfils us. It is why people climb tall buildings in every city around the world. I understand this is why Nimrod built the Tower of Babel, to be closer to God, both physically and to share the same perspective from the sky. This momentary experience of godlike perspective gives us an impression of *power*. It is why God punished Nimrod with the confusion of tongues that means we all speak different languages in this world (I don't subscribe to this Old Testament view). I believe it is why the powerful Rockefeller and Carnegie families built skyscrapers in New York. It is why armies build observation towers to gain a better perspective and therefore advantage over others.

What can this change of perspective tell us about love? Well, very little that we haven't already covered. Understanding someone else has a great deal to do with 'seeing things from their perspective'. But perhaps there is something else to consider. The snail sticks to the surface whatever the gradient, which could be a metaphor for sticking with a relationship and persevering with the difficult conditions you may encounter. In a more abstract way, we could consider the snail's climbing of walls to symbolise that relationships should adapt with their terrain, and new obstacles should be overcome instead of trying to stay on an even keel. I love hearing about the people who have been married for many, many years and I wonder what obstacles they overcame. I shudder at the idea that their lives may have simply been pedestrian and they had nothing to overcome. It is not because I fancy an adventurous lifestyle of drama and high-jinx; but I believe life is about new experiences informing our personal understanding of the world around us. Denying or rejecting new experiences is like a snail that only wants to stay on the ground; it is possible but limited. Some people may think that I am being snobbish or belittling 'normality', and they may personally aspire to achieve a state of comfortable normality, to reduce uncertainty and to increase security. Great. If you know what you like and you are happy to stick to it, I applaud you. I am not on some constant quest to discover new things because I am unhappy with what I have. I do not seek new experiences just to remain stimulated and interested in life. I believe that life throws up situations that challenge normalcy, and relationships should be dynamic enough to survive these extreme moments, not through psychological denial ("it never happened!"), but with emotional maturity ("let's talk about it"). Relationships should be able to embrace whatever change occurs, be it the death of a loved one or the unexpected birth of another. Life is difficult and people should be prepared for such challenges. Stereotypically the English prefer the denial, in some perverse stoical stiff-upper-lip behaviour that means we don't show emotional vulnerability. Recently this has changed with the public 'outpouring' of emotion over the death of Diana (or going out of international football tournaments on penalties). Neither response shows emotional maturity and is more about a communal reaction to something that had very little personal impact on their life. Why not deal with the real challenges when they arise in a relationship? Well, you can deal with challenges when they arise, but it often isn't the time to discover someone's true sense of character. If someone has a weakness in their ability to cope with any given situation, you'd be happier knowing about it so you can either avoid these situations or support them through it. Perhaps encouraging change for change's sake is not necessary, but understanding that life will change, and people will change and therefore relationships will change is an important realisation. Anyone who wants to argue that people and societies do not fundamentally change should take their conservatism and get re-educated. Whilst we may be governed by fundamental characteristics like the survival instinct, I believe we would change our habitats pretty quickly if our survival depended upon it. It is the one who is slow to adapt that is at risk. Being in a dynamic relationship that can cope with obstacles increases the likelihood of longevity methinks, purely because it has the capacity to deal with extremity. How can you prepare a relationship for the real challenges? I believe it is about being a dynamic individual. Let me clarify what I mean by that. I do not mean dynamic in the sense of a process, characterised by constant change, activity or progress. It is impossible to love someone who doesn't have any constancy, as it is difficult to determine his or her real character and identity. I mean dynamic in the sense of a person, positive in attitude and full of energy and new ideas. I don't believe these characteristics are essential, as I know of plenty of relationships that survive out of sheer bloody-mindedness and the fear of being alone, but this is not a very pleasant way of living in the long-term in my opinion.

The sharp minded amongst you will have noticed that I am not in a qualified position to comment on successful relationships when I openly admitted in the beginning that I embarked on this project as a result of being bad in relationships. You have a couple of choices. You can either ignore what I've been writing and do the exact opposite, in the hope that it will lead to a successful relationship. Or you can assume that whilst I believe this is how relationships should be hypothetically conducted, I am actually useless in reality in executing my feelings. I believe the latter is true. I believe that my approach to relationships is similar to the British transport system. I am built for the average day not the whole continuum of weather conditions. This is not dynamic. I have been a fair-weather friend and a fickle lover. It took some time watching snails to recognise this.

5.3. The representation of snails:

Having explored the physiology and behaviour of snails, it is now time to turn to their representation.

5.3.1. Snails as a pest:

My wonderful Gugga, a devout Christian, used to sing in church on a Sunday:

'All things bright and beautiful,
all creatures great and small,
all things wise and wonderful,
the Lord God made them all.'

Then he went home to crush snails in his garden hours later. This hypocrisy was strange to me as a child, even though I didn't know what hypocrisy was at that point. I found it unusual that we were celebrating 'each little flower that opens' and then stamping the life out of snails. Were these God's accidents? Did God not intend for snails to be here? The meaning of hypocrisy only came apparent to me a few years later when in school, but I retrofitted it to Gugga's actions. To be hypocritical is to claim you have a moral standard and then not living up to it yourself. Institutional religion has since been exposed to have plenty of double standards, so Gugga was only really acting in the tradition of his church[10]. Snails ate his lettuce, which meant they were pests. A disruptive force. I don't think he ever had second thoughts about whether there was a moral contradiction in crushing them. I'm sure he would have justified it somehow by quoting from some part of the big book, where JC crushed a snail to save a leper or something equally ludicrous. A juncture occurred at this moment and several realisations dawned on me (an epiphany if you will):

1) I didn't like everything about Gugga,
2) He didn't truly believe in everything he sang about in church,
3) I began to like snails.

---

[10] Thank God he was only a snail-crushing hypocrite instead of a child molesting one. In all fairness to Gugga, he was a wonderful person who I loved very much, and the snail crushing was about as evil as he got in my experience. I miss him a lot.

The first point is a painful one. Whilst I loved everything else about this wonderful man, I didn't like this. There is a lot written about the point that a parent goes from loving their child unconditionally until the love becomes conditional upon good behaviour etcetera. I believe the same is true of a child's love for their parents. It is initially unconditional, as adults are infallible. Then chasms open up when the child realises that certain actions or sayings are incongruous with everything else, and the adult becomes fallible. When this realisation occurs it is a deflating experience, because the bedrock of everything becomes rocked to the core, a personal paradigm shift. I didn't like the way that Gugga crushed snails. I felt it differed from what he preached and sang about in church. He went down in my estimation, and so did church. My reaction was a strange one; I began to like snails. Why? I had previously been indifferent to these slimy creatures, so why did I start caring for them at this point? I believe that I liked what they represented, not what they actually were. They weren't really pests, they were just creatures. They were pests in relation to Gugga, because they undermined his effort to grow lettuce. The word 'pest' only refers to something that is destructive in relation to humans. It's a word that is applied to anything that challenges our dominant position as ruler of the animal kingdom. This snail crushing alerted me to the fact that 'actions speak louder than words', and whilst God made all creatures bright and beautiful he also gave humans carte blanche to crush anything that didn't suit their own needs and wants. Crushed snails helped me realise Gugga's infallibility (especially surrounding religion), and for that I would always be grateful. From that moment on, I was quietly happy when they ate through his lettuce and annoyed him. Personally I hated eating lettuce, so snails weren't pests to me as they were doing me a favour. I loved the fact they were underdogs, a disruptive mischief that could frustrate a grown man. This inspired me. Throughout my time in school I became a subversive nuisance, not gratuitously, but enough to agitate my teachers. Agitation wasn't the goal; I was interested in challenging the status quo and the fundamental assumptions that we were being taught. I was the annoying student who always asked 'why?' in an attempt to dig deeper into understanding something. The majority of my teachers were stressed into teaching us a national curriculum that they needed us to learn by rote. If it wasn't going to turn up in the exam, you didn't need to learn it, regardless of whether you were interested. Far from empowering us with the tools of enquiry and effective research that would enable life-long learning, we were encouraged to 'cram' disparate pieces of knowledge in order to regurgitate it at a later point. Disrupting the teacher's didactic flow of information was punishable with detentions and bad reports. I therefore lost interest in school.

I hate to think that I am encouraging nuisance for its own sake, but I guess I am. Whilst there is nothing more annoying than a noisy contrary pest in the corner of a room disagreeing with everything that the majority agrees on, I believe there is a need for the devil's advocate. Challenging and provoking the accepted paradigm was an essential part of Enlightenment thinking. Whilst logic and reason may be crude tools for analysis, I value them above the traditional, superstitious or dogmatic. The challenge comes when we have to recognise the difference between the contentious and the contrary people, which often descends into a subjective decision. I cannot propose a solution to this problem, but I do believe that listening to the disparate voices, however frustrating, is better than not allowing everyone to speak. After all, the Lord God made them all! That said; perpetual theoretical challenges could lead to the stagnation of action and paralysis through analysis that I wrote of earlier. This is not dissimilar to the process of filibustering in American politics, where an individual can prolong a debate for so long that no vote or action can be taken on the topic; an academic form of timewasting. The bipartisan politics during Obama's presidency seems to have been mired by opponents refusing to ratify anything substantial and led to a deadlock in decision-making. I believe that these impasses are perhaps inevitable within political systems, but I believe in the notion of constructive action, whereby people should try to offer pragmatic, compromising solutions instead of blanket vetoes. I'm sure there will be people reading who think this is idealist twaddle and completely impractical. Such is life; you cannot be all things to all people.

Back to Gugga. It was not so much the death of the snails as much as the manner with which it was done. I have already said that I was indifferent to the snails, but it was his inhumane method of destroying them that was incongruous with his religious views.

Where was the compassion? The benevolence? I believe he interpreted the Bible to be kind to his brothers and sisters, but felt snails fell out of the remit of the humanity that Jesus spoke of. Noah was obviously a dunce for letting snails on the ark, as he could have solved Gugga's problem ages ago. Had Gugga left a beer trap for the snails, and they had crawled in of their own volition, he probably could have given me a really good lesson about vice, greed and alcoholism.[11] An opportunity missed perhaps?

In love, a pest or nuisance is difficult. In the same way that a child can rebel against their parents, I believe lovers can rebel against one another. What are the forces behind such behaviour? Is there an influence that one lover is forcing on the other? This is perhaps a good question to ask yourself if you encounter a pest for a lover. One thing is for sure; you cannot perpetually endure a pest. Whilst occasional disruption is likely when two people are in a relationship, if it is disproportionately difficult then the relationship is destructive and pointless. Don't stick with the things that make you overwhelmingly unhappy. This is where it is difficult for parents, because some children can seem like a perpetual pest and you have to stick with them! But your relationship is different. A child is forever a product of what you brought in to the world. If you have a problem with how they've turned out, there is probably a long, hard look to be taken at yourself at some point. Lovers are different, as they bring their histories and issues into the relationship, and sometimes it is nothing to do with you whatsoever.

My conclusion is that pests are a personal challenge to us. They should make us question our own position and beliefs. Use the opportunity to reflect. What is the best way of dealing with the disruption? Crushing snails is possible, but can you control children with the same conviction when they will ultimately grow and become independent? Have mercy with pests, and try to treat them as humanely as possible. As the violent book says: 'do as you would be done unto'.

---

[11] A digression. Is a beer trap okay then? And if so, can it be used for pesky lovers?

5.3.2. Snails as food:

There is a further reason for finding Gugga's snail crushing disappointing, as snails are eaten on the continent and he couldn't stand the idea of wasting food. Whilst I would have undoubtedly found the process of eating snails disgusting as a child (I still struggle to think about it now), I would've been accepting of the fact that he found them in the garden and ate them. We went searching in the rock pools for shrimp at the seaside and I'd consider that to be no different.

So, snails are considered to be food in some places. What can this teach us about life? It is really easy to think of ourselves as indestructible creatures, with all our medicines, but ultimately we are meat also. Our lives are moments of consciousness that we are desperate to inject meaning into. There is always a sense of sadness when a human dies earlier than we consider 'natural', despite the fact that death is all part of nature. Dying of 'natural causes' is a strange expression. A car accident is not considered to be a natural cause (because it is often humankind that created the accident) yet the human is part of nature, and driving erratically could be part of someone's 'nature'. We have to console ourselves that the deceased will return into the ecosystem either as ashes or through decomposition, and we believe the consciousness is over. It is their consciousness that we often miss the most when he or she dies. We miss their humour, their character. We mourn the loss of what the individual meant to *us*. Grieving has a perfectly acceptable selfish element, whereby we lament the loss that we feel ourselves. They are gone and we are still here, confronting the world without them. Tragedy is attached when we believe they 'had a life ahead of them', and we grieve the loss of their potential. This is particularly difficult to cope with when the young die, as we feel their innocence compounds the tragedy. Pain, sorrow and suffering accompany the loss and it seems that there will be no possible healer, except time perhaps. It is little consolation to know that their body returns into the ecosystem. But the fact remains that we are all earthly beings and we will all die, one way or another, and the cycle looks set to repeat itself, for the near future at least. A snail can be a pest. They can be gourmet in the 'developed' world or a necessary source of proteins in poor countries. The potential for the snail is varied, but their death is still a death. Crushed, fried with garlic, old age; they die in different ways but they still die. We are all the same.

What about creativity? I think using snails within meals is pretty creative. Cooking is on a continuum whereby it can be a creative past time or simply a functional necessity in our lives. Personally I find the temporality of a dish such a shame that I favour function over form (as I mentioned earlier). I like it to taste good and fill me up. It's all going to be digested soon anyway. Obviously others may disagree. They consider presentation to be a big part of the process. If you want to notice the seismic difference in the continuum, it is most noticeable in fast food restaurants where the food is nowhere near the pornographic representation on the menu. No one cares because we usually want the food to rid us of our immediate hunger. Either way, the presentation of food is not the only form of creativity. Whilst presentation may appeal to the sense of sight, cooking lets us create different tastes and smells too, which must be a fantastical palette to play with. I imagine the meal sits beside films, books, paintings or songs as a *form*, and the ingredients and their relationship to one another are the *composition*. There are so many variables of different ingredients in different quantities, cooked in different ways. It is a truly creative past time, yet temporal, whereby a fleeting moment of pleasure must pass over the chef much like the performer on the stage after the curtain comes down. A momentary high, before it is all over, perhaps to be recreated again. It may be better next time, it may be worse. It may be similar, but it will rarely be the same again. This is the bittersweet side of such temporal creativity.

What can snails as food teach us about love? Well, we can joke that the most obvious thing is that anything sounds sexy if it is said in French, even edible snails. The *escargot* sounds more appealing to the Anglophone; primarily because of the French accent and secondly because the English word is phonetically close to nail with the slimy, slithering 'S' stuck on the front. It doesn't sound alluring at all. Whilst I'm not suggesting everyone should learn French to woo his or her lover, I do think language plays an important part in finding a partner. Hidden in our spoken words are a context that displays our temperament, our intellectual and emotional intelligence and our beliefs. Our intonation can alter meaning, influencing suggestibility or persuasion. Whilst articulate people can control and manipulate their language, others are sometimes lost for words at the point that they need them most. This takes us back to the discussion on function and form. I mentioned earlier that I'm not a perfectionist but a pragmatist. I personally take the same approach to language and I don't get too upset surrounding the rules of grammar. However, I do get annoyed when a word is used in a wrong context, as the language hasn't then performed the *function* of communicating. I once had a lecturer who believed that American literature focussed on actions and narrative rather than the European preference for character and form. 'He said' or 'she said' were sufficient instead of 'he insinuated' and 'she acquiesced'. My lecturer felt that the European approach distracted from the storytelling as opposed to supporting it. If we use the analogy of a snail as food, it may be pretty indigestible when taken straight from the garden, but tasty when cooked in garlic. The form that the snail takes makes the function of eating it more or less desirable. The point is that this comes down to personal preference, and whilst language has rules, I believe it is perfectly fine to break them. It annoys me that we would hail Shakespeare a genius for shaving off syllables to reach a certain iambic pentameter yet we would chastise a teenager for shortening words to save SMS characters. Personally it doesn't matter as long as the correct meaning gets across.

Similarly, I am not a fan of fashion. I like to place the emphasis on personality. However, many people do consider image and fashion to be important. People 'dress up' to become "tasty", just like the snails being cooked in garlic.

I've digressed from love. People like to eat snails in different ways and some people don't like eating snails at all. Love is all about personal preference and we shouldn't have to justify our decisions to anyone but ourselves.

5.3.3. Snail mail:

Snail mail is the derogatory term given to postal services in the physical world of atoms as opposed to electronic mail (email). It coined the term snail mail because it is slow in comparison. Mail is one of the victims in our instantaneous culture of communication. I am fortunate enough to remember the last halcyon years of love letters before text messages, emails and Facebook tags became ubiquitous. The arrival of post was wonderful as a child because it either signified an impending celebration like birthday or Christmas, or because it was a rare correspondence from someone you knew or occasionally something unique from a company or suchlike. Nowadays, the only way to achieve occasional excitement through the post is to order some shopping online, as most of my post is predominately requests for payment or a notification that I am overdrawn. Which reminds me, we should look at some more of the papier-mâché snails. After all, they were snail mail letters, pulped down into snails that travelled slowly around the world.

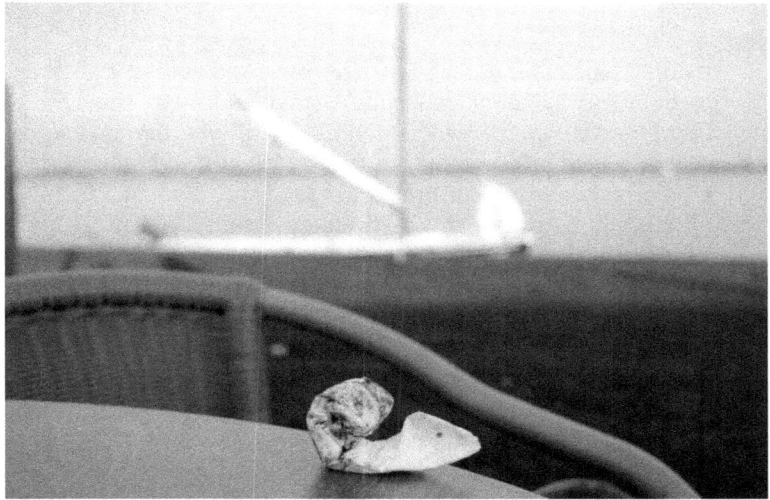

Joe in Friesland, Netherlands

Mail isn't the only thing that gets chastised for being slow. In the increasingly rapid world in which we live, slow drivers get harangued on the roads and slow walkers get hassled on the pavements. I guess this all comes from the stimulation that surrounds us. There are lots of things to do and lots to get done, so we don't want to waste time. The problem is that not everyone can move at that speed, and the elderly and infirm get swept aside in the undertow. In the technological era, if anything operates slowly it is a sign of age. In the technological era, 'new' is the best and age is only valued for nostalgic reasons, when it can be repackaged and resold to us as 'retro'. Everything should be upgraded, made new and fast. A few things have created a virtue out of old age, some alcohol for example, which can be seen as mature or vintage. However, this vintage works as an asset through reputation or brand. Like 'retro', 'vintage' is fine as a brand. If age is not perceived to be an asset, it is a nuisance. Experience and wisdom are obviously assets, but only if they can be applied to our modern living. Having experience of a different time with different paradigms doesn't necessarily woo the youth.[12] This lack of concern for the elderly is commonly cited as the reason that most first-world families put their elderly relatives into a home instead of bringing them back into the family for their final years, which is quite common in other cultures.

I don't particularly fear old age, but I do worry that we are a technologically fetishized culture that embraces the new for no other reason than *newness*. Even now, at the tender age of 32, I don't possess or crave the latest technology and I believe there is a whole section of culture that I'm not participating in. The ubiquitous nature of this technology means I am probably losing necessary life skills that will prevent my own technological obsolescence in the paradigm shift. I'm not exaggerating. As a filmmaker, the industry is floundering around searching for a new business model now that scarcity has gone and so many screens compete for our attention. As a lecturer, the higher education system is floundering because it is expensive and requires a commitment that puts many people off and besides, it is possible to do many free online courses with some of the best lecturers in the world. I can scream that the learning experience is not the same, and scream that watching a movie on your laptop is not the same

---

[12] Personally I find it fascinating when I meet anyone from a different part of the world who has lived under a different political system from democracy. I'm full of questions.

as in a cinema, but culture is changing. Even now amongst my friends, I witness the lamentation that things are not the same as they used to be. Is this the conversation that the lock keepers had beside the canal as the train whizzed past? Is this the conversation that train drivers had as the motorways were being built? Is this the conversation that postal workers had as the Internet arrived in our homes? The sadness is, we do not seem any closer to the leisure society that this technology was meant to bring about. Instead, it seems we must find new jobs and careers to fulfil and fund our lives. Ironically, I believe we are witnessing a few people who creatively adapt to this technological era by deliberately developing vintage or small batch products that can be cost effective with a global audience instead of the limitations of the physical high street. I wonder whether some creative person will make handwriting cool again and we'll see a return to snail mail? I don't think that this emphasis on newness is any different from the past, for as long as society is preoccupied on the acquisition of consumer goods, society will value *newness*. Keeping up with the neighbours. Periodically the emphasis will change, from quality, to innovation, to style. Keeping in fashion requires popular consumption and popular trends. Obviously fashion can be broken into many sub-sections. I am fashionable on the basis that I take a shower every day, which was not the case 200 years ago. But I'm not fashionable in the sense that I don't possess a smartphone or have a tattoo. In this sense, I am not a trendsetter. I wait to see whether a fad is going to stick around and then I'll try to make a sturdy investment on the basis of what will last me the longest. This could be equated as being a tight-ass, but I don't see the point of changing something if I have no need to. Which is where advertising comes in. It is the purpose of advertising to convince you that you have a need for their product. Their job is to play upon your wants, needs and desires to purchase stuff. All of this manipulation must take place within the boundaries that society finds acceptable. For example, young women on the front of lad-magazines and spread across page three of the most popular newspaper mean that the objectification of women within our society is acceptable. Will people of the future look at our media as if we were some emancipated society that scoffed at other patriarchal cultures who insisted their women be hidden under a burka? Or will we look like hypocrites that kept a patriarchal culture of men in top jobs, using scantily clad women to sell magazines and papers, to a society of people who believed they were equal because the women didn't have to wear a burka? This is my problem with *newness*; it is a constant distraction from deeper issues. There is a whole host of inequitable traditions that pervade our society and yet most people act unaware, or unconcerned by the inequity. Fashion is about telling you your needs, your wants and a whole host of individual concerns with yourself, all connected to how the rest of society perceives you. Community can be a fashionable topic, but I believe that building a successful community requires much stronger foundations of trust. I believe friendships require the same foundations. I believe these foundations require time and shared experiences. I'm not advocating a mass return to snail mail, but contemplating the postal service makes me believe that we shouldn't get distracted by *newness*; the constant noise of new information, new films, new music, new fashions. Writing letters didn't have the same homogenous experience of email. I love email as it performs the function of communication effectively. But I get a lot of email that is sent without thought or consideration. Letters didn't seem to have this problem, as even a scribbled note required a stamp and a visit to a post box. It is that consideration that I think is sometimes missing with *newness* and I think we could do with a little more.

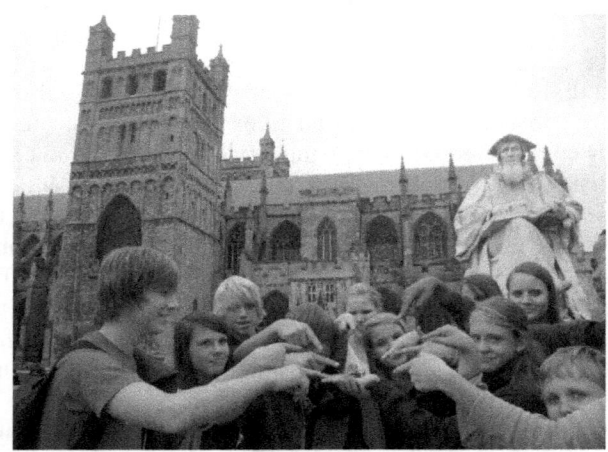

Fran in Exeter, with a lot of enthusiastic German tourists

5.3.4. Snail trail:

A 'snail trail' is the slang expression for the abdominal hair between the belly button and the pubic hair surrounding your genitals. At this point I must admit that I am struggling to see how this can be used as an analogy for anything. It is also known as the 'happy line' and the 'treasure trail', which I guess are names given by fans of the sagittal pattern of hair, as 'snail trail' suggests something slimy and small is at the end of the line.[13] Once again, we are reminded that we live in a diverse world, and we all like different things.

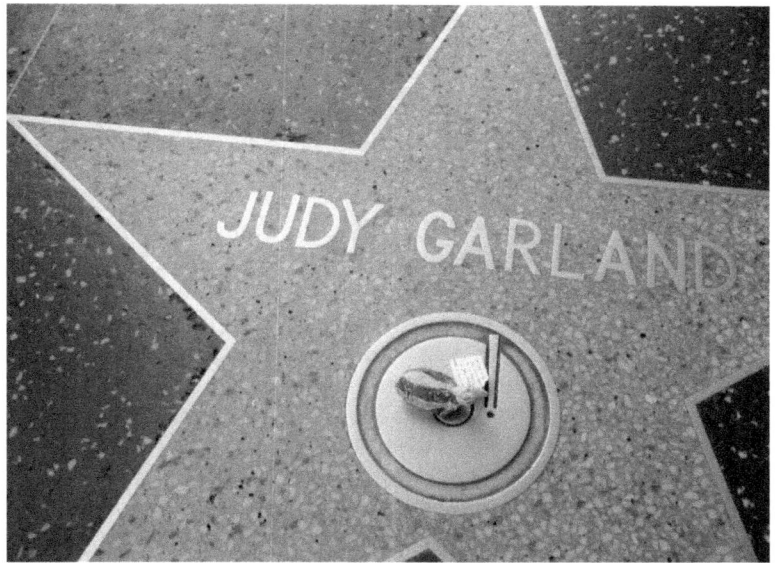

Sammy in LA, darling

---

[13] My editor drew a little picture in the margin of the draft copy that I sent him. It was a rough sketch of a penis and how it resembles the shape of a snail when considered with the testicles. Imagine the balls to be a shell, and the penis to be the body of the snail. I'm not including the picture because it really changes the tone of the book in my opinion. Suffice to say, I was in awe of the imagination that this analogy required.

5.3.5. Snails as a sexual fetish:

I believe I am saving the best till last. Having reminded you that we live in a diverse world and we all like different things, it should come as no surprise that snails are seen as a sexual fetish. Personally I was not aware of this until I registered the Crushing Snails website, and noticed that a lot of traffic to the site was from people searching for snails being crushed in socks, or snails being crushed by women in heels. I'm not particularly fascinated with the fetish per se, but I am fascinated at which point the individual discovered they had this particular fetish. What were they doing when they realised this is what excited them? I have a genuine curiosity about this. What is the point at which we realise that we like something? Must we be open to the experience of trying something new before we can know whether we like it or not? Surely we don't all have to crush snails in our socks before deciding that it is not for us? We can visualise and imagine, predicting what our reaction will be like.

I spent the large part of my childhood doing this, mostly with food. My mum would despair when I said 'I don't like that' after barely trying it. Olives, fish, avocado, parsnips, broad beans, sprouts. On reflection this wasn't a long list, as it could be paraphrased by saying 'vegetables and fish', but that is quite a broad part of the food spectrum. Besides, it isn't strictly true, as there were exceptions too, like fish fingers and baked beans. The point is, we close the door to lots of experiences in life before ever getting the chance to experience them, some people more than others. Sometimes this is due to opportunity, other times it is due to preference. Either way, if we believe that we are shaped by our experiences, we are all different by the simple fact that no one has seen exactly what you have seen, in the combination that you saw it. It is all subject to the wooliness of personal judgement. What one person sees as suitable, another disagrees. Whereas we are largely free to pursue whatever route we personally choose, sometimes conflict arises where decisions are intertwined with another person who has their own differing opinions. Parents, lovers, employers and friends all influence us. It is at these points, when our ideas, choices and desires intersect with the people around us, that we open ourselves up to being judged by others, whether we like it or not. It is these moments when our attitudes to one another really count, because this is the point that we have the potential to crush the dreams and ideas of others. I'm not going to profess that we can move towards a time in future whereby this doesn't happen. I believe this collision of ideas and beliefs is a flaw within humanity, and no amount of wishful thinking will make it disappear. It is far more likely that we can condition ourselves to cope with these experiences when they occur to us than eradicate their happening. This is simply because we all make judgements towards others ourselves, and is it easier to ignore judgements directed towards us than we are at preventing the (sometimes unconscious) judgements we make of others. Therefore we cannot refuse others to have their judgement of us, but to consider whether their judgement is valuable in relation to our own, positively or negatively. It is a complex process that involves so many variables, most notably; how much do you care for their opinion and how much is at stake?[14] Coping with these judgements is something we just have to deal with, and I can offer no advice on how that works. Ultimately I believe that *judgement* is the point at which life, love and creativity all become complex, as our personal decisions and choices must be exposed to the thoughts of others if we are to succeed in love and life, and will have to be exposed to others should we wish to gain recognition for our creativity.

---

[14] Perhaps this is why the end of the world is considered by some to be the Last Judgement? As if our actions will be considered by some entity (in accordance with their belief system) as to whether we have been right or wrong during our lifetime. I'm sure Saddam Hussein had an opinion on this, judging by his refusal to acknowledge the legitimacy of his trial, which sparked wide condemnation and disapproval from much of the world. In his case the judgement resulted in his execution, which it is difficult for him to personally ignore. It sucks if the judge doesn't share your world-view, a fact that led me to reject Pascal's Wager, preferring to be godless rather than backing God only find that it is Allah on the other side.

6. Conclusions:

Snails simply *exist*. Although I have spent an entire book attaching meaning to their existence, they are ultimately meaningless (we are too). Perhaps you'd be more successful in love, life and creativity if you didn't try over examining and attaching meaning to everything. Accept that things are what they are and let that liberate you. Searching for meaning can become debilitating to the point that you over-analyse everything and search for meaning where there is none. Similarly, don't make goals in your love, life or creativity. Love, life and creativity are not destinations; they are all journeys. They shouldn't have definitive conclusions. They should all be approached with an open mind. Sometimes when we fix our eyes on certain goals we miss the other opportunities around us. I'm not sure that snails have ambitions or goals to contend with.

Scrapping your ambitions seems a ludicrous suggestion, because we are taught that 'aimless' and 'unambitious' are poor character virtues. I'm not suggesting that you scrap your aims, but that you don't let them disadvantage you by blinding you to other options or possibilities. In *Black Swans*, Nicholas Nassim Taleb wrote about how you only miss a train if you were intending to catch it. That is the pain of missing your projected aim. Now, you may be late, which may have other consequences, but you are not dead. Similarly, you won't die when you are on time and the train is late. Get some perspective. Just because it didn't meet your expectations, don't let it *anger* you. It is out of your control. It just exists. I think this is what upsets car drivers so much, because the freedom of a car should equate to being able to be a decision maker in your route to work. But when traffic is bad and there are no car parking places, it seems like a personal defeat. It is what it is. Live with it and be at peace with it. Your life will be less stressful. You will have happier relationships if you carry no expectation of one another. You will have a far more creative experience if you are freed from expectation.

It is difficult to behave in such a carefree way because much of our education and upbringing is set upon aims and objectives. "What do you want to be when you grow up?" is perhaps one of the stupidest questions to ask a child. Adults enjoy the youthful, ambitious naïve responses, primarily because children aren't cynical. You don't hear a caring four-year old child say that they would like to be a nurse but the understaffing of wards and constant bureaucracy makes it unappealing. They are not in a position to know what they'd like to be when they grow up. Aside from the innocent answers, I think that adults only ask children about their futures in an attempt to provide for it. We want the next generation to have whatever they need in order to get on and succeed in life. However, sometimes the pressure can have an adverse effect. Not meeting your own expectations of yourself is insufferable enough, but not meeting the expectations of others is equally bad.

We live in a society were many of the pressures that are placed upon us are not part of the physical world of nature. Most of our stresses are human constructs and we would do well to remember them as such. Your ambition is only useful if it makes you happy in some way, like some sense of achievement. If it doesn't make you happy, jettison it. Ambition is only useful if it gives you a sense of purpose, or a goal to work towards that gives you *meaning* and *comfort* in your life. If it doesn't, jettison it. Realise that aims and ambitions should only be applied in a personal context, and you are destined for failure on the occasions where your aims and ambitions are designed for others (this is known more commonly as *politics*). However, this is a very individualistic way of thinking, and it makes you sound like a pessimist. It is the involvement of others that makes love, life and creativity so complex. Perhaps your life is about searching for the people who will be open to your ideas on love, life and creativity, and valuing those people once you find them. I don't know.

It is difficult to draw such a sprawling and random study of such complex themes into any sensible and coherently meaningful conclusion. It was never the intention, as I noted in the rationale that I simply wanted to reflect upon the issues as opposed to concluding with a neat solution. I'm sorry it offers no sweet resolution, ironically I believe this **is** the conclusion; such things can never be resolved. Relationships and individual lives may have their distinct timelines and end at some stage, but love, life and creativity are seemingly in perpetuity.[15] Neatly tying up these complex issues would arguably bring an end to the one thing that gives life a purpose. Solving love, life and creativity would delete our reason for being. Maybe we constructed these things to give ourselves meaning. Maybe life is just about organisms and genes looking to expand their empires, but that doesn't detract from the fact that it has provided us with an excellent by-product. We have *consciousness*, the state of being aware. This study has encouraged me to celebrate consciousness, as I genuinely believe that I am guilty of negating my senses. I damage my consciousness with alcohol and distractions. I think I am aware whilst I am actually unaware. Let's be honest, sometimes the pursuit of understanding is exhausting and it is easier to be ignorant. Ignorance is the line of least resistance. Perhaps our wilful ignorance is because most of us feel that the world's problems seem so plentiful and that our own impact is negligible in the grand scheme of things. What difference can I make? The question should be 'what difference can we make?' and collectively, even if operating in isolation, the effect could be quite large. Think of the papier-mâché snails. Making and sharing them is only the beginning; individual people finding them, taking photos and sharing them with everyone else creates something special. Collectively recycling, collectively contributing to charities, all of these things require individuals working together to make an impact.

Modestly belittling your own contribution to a better society is one thing, belittling it to the point where you do nothing is foolish. I find it tragic that some people value themselves so little that they don't believe they can make a difference. I believe these frustrations are the catalysts for depression, and we now medically recognise the symptoms to be debilitating. Some suggest that we should rebrand depression as 'unhappiness' and tell everyone to accept it as part of life, but I think that is crass. Depression is much more than unhappiness; it is a feeling of worthlessness. Severe depression can reach the stage where even happiness seems pointless. I think we need to look at what things within our society

---

[15] I use the caveat of 'seemingly' as we should not take our eternal existence for granted. If life is a necessary pre-requisite for love and creativity then we will need to survive as a species in order for all three to continue (not that any human will care at that stage if everything has gone).

truly make us happy, and what things are impacting upon the happiness of others? This is the moment that requires true reflection and honesty, bywords for analysis and evaluation. Happiness doesn't have to be equated with fun or playfulness. Happiness can come from fairness and equality, and the sense that you are neither being suppressed by outside forces or acting as a suppressor of someone else. Happiness can also be the moments when you are almost lost to the outside world, so absorbed in something that you enjoy and take pleasure in, 'losing' ourselves in the moment, unaware of the time. Obviously I am being idealistic and it is unlikely that all of the world's woes will be eradicated in our lifetime, but that doesn't mean that we shouldn't strive for the improvement![16]

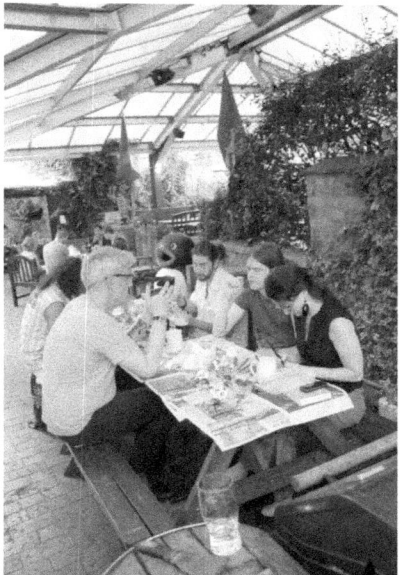

Painting with friends doesn't happen often enough

---

[16] "Ah! I thought you preferred imperfection, as it is the character of something? How come you are now suggesting we try for a perfect world?" Actually, I argued that we should try to improve the function if we can, and the form is less important.

Why is happiness so important? Well I believe happiness is the key to love, life and creativity. I believe it is difficult to engage with any of the three unless you are in pursuit of happiness. Ultimately, I believe a fixed state of happiness is unattainable and undesirable; bad things will always happen at some point or another. But I believe it is the ability to recognise what makes you happy (and the ability to recognise *when* you are *truly* happy also) that can drive you forward to achieve great things in love, life and creativity.

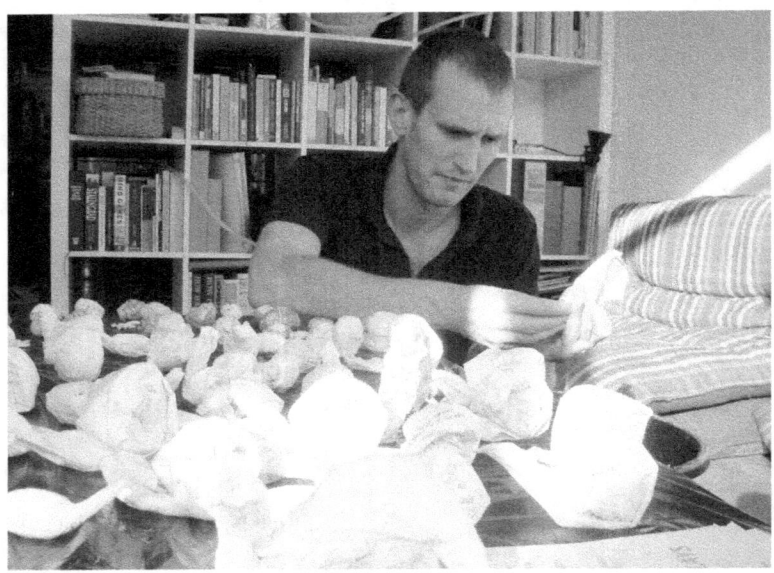

Turning my bank overdraft into snails

About the author:

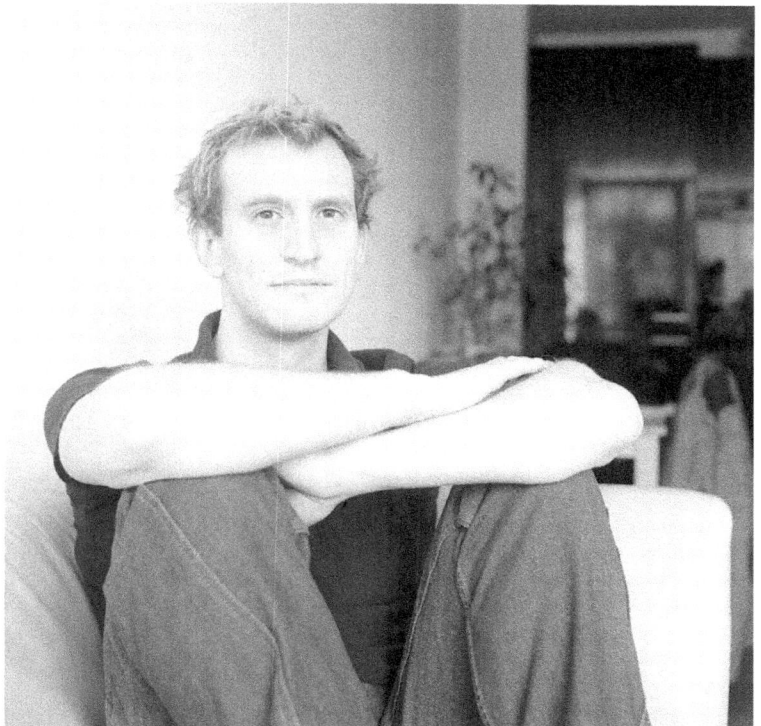

Photo by Ian Jones

I began writing book reviews for my local newspaper when I was 12, but the screen in the corner of the room distracted me. By the age of 22 I had directed and produced a series of documentaries about nightshift workers for Channel Four. I have since written lots of scripts and turned a few of them in to films. As well as being a filmmaker I have worked as an academic, film production consultant, sound recordist, runner, teddy bear stuffer, bookseller, hi-fi salesman and paperboy. In my spare time I have attempted to be a musician, a blogger, a bon vivant and a masterful lover. I have had differing levels of success in each of these fields, but I won't tell you which is which.

www.ingramcontent.com/pod-product-compliance
Lightning Source LLC
Chambersburg PA
CBHW072222170526
45158CB00002BA/711